DRESSAGE

DRESSAGE

An Approach to Competition

KATE HAMILTON

HOWELL BOOK HOUSE INC.
230 Park Avenue, New York, N.Y. 10169

Published 1987 by Howell Book House Inc.
230 Park Avenue, New York, N.Y. 10169

Reprinted 1988

Library of Congress Cataloging-in-Publication Data

Hamilton, Kate.
Dressage.

Includes index.
Summary: Describes the sport of dressage and how to train horses and prepare riders for dressage competitions.
1. Dressage. [1. Dressage. 2. Horsemanship. 3. Horses — Training] I. Title.
SF 309.5.H25 1987 798.2′3 86-27296
ISBN 0-87605-862-4

Dedicated to my father, Harry Keightley Robinson

Acknowledgements

My sincere thanks to my pupils who generously allowed me to ride their horses for some of the photographs. My special thanks to the following people for their kindness and hard work: Helene Panton who typed the manuscript; Kay Humphries, Pamela Yeomans, Linda Rush, Jade Derby and Karen Slaughter Evitt for their great help and support; Kit Houghton who produced the photographs and Mr W.R. Benyon MP who allowed us to use his beautiful deer park for the photographic work.

Line illustrations by Annette Findlay

Typeset by Alacrity Phototypesetters, Weston-super-Mare
Printed and bound in Great Britain
at the University Printing House, Oxford

Contents

1	The Dressage Rider	7
2	Choosing Your Dressage Horse	19
3	Fitness	43
4	Basic Training	55
5	The Competition World	73
6	Strengthening the Base	87
7	From Elementary to Medium	100
8	Medium Level	118
9	Flying Changes	130
10	Into Top Level	137
	Appendix Lunging and Longreining	142
	Index	158

1 The Dressage Rider

Any business partnership which intends to survive the test of time needs some essential basic ingredients. Motivation and energy may give a new project a good start, but equally important in the long term is a sound knowledge of the skills involved: understanding, decision-making and communication.

A good dressage partnership is no exception to this rule. If you are aiming to build up a successful working relationship with a young horse, his initial contribution to your project is likely to be energy – probably of a volcanic nature – but little skill. Even the most promising partner, in possession of a naturally good outline and paces, can only expect to be successful in competition through novice and elementary levels. His natural ability, without help from a straight and effective rider, will usually run out when medium level work is demanded, because it has no real foundations.

Those foundations must be laid by you. Every horse can only perform as well as his rider, so before you can even begin to work with your new partner, you will need to understand the essential qualities of a good dressage rider.

The Skilled Rider

Many misconceptions surround the ability to ride well. One such belief is that the earlier a child sits on a saddle, the better he will be as a rider. This is rarely the case. Another is that an accomplished rider, whose silhouette cuts a clean line on the horse and whose technique is exceptional, is a 'natural'. Again, this is most unlikely. That rider may have a natural affinity with horses, but whether he is a show-jumping rider, a flat race jockey or a dressage expert, he arrived there through seeking knowledge, putting it into practice, and continually striving to improve his present performance – all very hard work!

In short, riders are made, not born, and the recipe is a remarkably simple one. A dressage rider and competitor is both an artist and a sportsman. In both capacities he requires singular control of mind and body. Comparisons here are revealing. Dressage relates closely to three performing arts, in both its visual aspect, and in their common ground of progressive and dedicated training. They are ballet, ice skating and gymnastics. Each of these disciplines requires of its pupils a posture or position which is the 'base', without which balanced movements from one exercise to another could not be accomplished.

The rider's position in the saddle is the equivalent base, or at least it should be. A clever rider may create the illusion that the horse can do it all without him, but this is the rider who has learned through thoughtful training and experience to feel on every horse he rides, in each pace and in all directions, whether he is remaining in balance in the middle of the saddle. Unfortunately, the majority of horses are generous to a fault, and learn to adapt to the position they are, literally, saddled with. The rider may be badly collapsed to the outside of the saddle, he may be behind the movement or ahead of it, but the horse will still have a go at the exercise demanded. This is because he has, through repetition, learned to respond to whatever set of aids his rider uses for the exercise. The ballet dancer moving without balance would fall over. Similarly, however co-operative his horse, this rider will reach a point where he has to go back to the drawing-board with his own position and aids, in order to recognise the restrictions he is imposing on his horse.

Fig 1 Dr Reine Klimke with his famous partner Ahleric.

Assessing Posture

It is essential that the rider appreciates the inherited, or acquired, weaknesses in his posture. We all favour the use of one hand, or pushing off with one leg; frequently we have one leg longer than the other. If the rider's body has also had its fair share of breakages, then simply standing up straight, in a level fashion, can necessitate concentration and correction. This may sound exaggerated, but I assure you it is not. When I am teaching competent riders in an advanced lunge lesson, I am able to assess the manner in which these riders carry themselves, even before they mount up.

Off the Horse

The starting point for your side of the partnership is to position yourself in front of a full-length mirror! Stand naturally – don't cheat by correcting dropped or very rounded shoulders or back before you have had an honest perusal. This exercise will tell you some of the details of your posture and the rest can be discovered by walking past some large shop windows. Keep walking and look sideways at your profile. Is your head dropped down? Your upper body tipped forward?

This is always an eye-opening experience. We all think we stand and walk well because usually when we check our appearance in a mirror, we have unconsciously preened ourselves first. Once you have examined your profile in action, I would hazard a guess that you will not be at all satisfied with what you discover.

Correction Firstly, don't forget how much you disliked your posture in action. Secondly, start analysing which parts of your anatomy have lazily crept out of their true alignment, and why that has happened.

If you have had any broken bones, then you may have to live with an unlevel shoulder or hip. It is, however, encouraging that osteopaths and physiotherapists are now very strict about getting sportsmen to work on their bodies and persuade injured parts to return to as near full working capacity as possible.

There is also a method of posture correction available called the Alexander Technique. This has proved useful to many performers in spheres such as music, acting and sport, where stressful conditions can lead to poor posture which then adversely affects performance. The technique teaches the pupil to regain the correct alignment of his body, reducing tension and aches caused by bad posture.

The will-power required for good deportment is an all-important factor, whether you go it alone or attend an exercise group. Having pin-pointed the root of your posture problems, set yourself some short and long-term goals. These might include:

1. Daily checks on deportment, sitting, standing and walking.
2. Daily exercises to ease stiffness (*see* Chapter 3).
3. A diary date one month from now to do the 'shop window' test.
4. Another diary date three months from now to have a video taken of your riding, in order to assess the improvement.

If you are likely to make the excuse that you have no time to do this, make an appointment with yourself every day and write the time in your diary.

On the Horse

Serious dressage riders appreciate that their position in the saddle, and its effect through legs and reins, is the key factor in the sound, progressive training of any horse. Strangely enough, however, the adverse influence and far-reaching effects of the rider's bad habits are not taken very seriously. Here is an example of an everyday situation, illustrating how easily problems can begin and grow.

Visualise two horses working on a twenty-metre circle, in trot on the left rein. The first rider has good rhythm, he sits in the centre of the saddle, with his horse working forward between both legs and reins. The horse is bent around

Fig 2 Anne Grethe Jenson with Marzog, showing a secure, effective and elegant position in the saddle.

the rider's inside leg, working from that bend into a secure outside rein contact. The rider's outside leg is effective in controlling that side of the horse, and ensuring that he stretches forward through his outside shoulder with controlled impulsion.

Now picture the other horse, of equal natural ability. This horse's rider collapses the left side of his body, causing his seat to move across the saddle to the right. His left side is weak and the right rein contact has become light and intermittent. The collapsed left side has made the rider's left leg reasonably effective, but contributes to a 'floating' right leg. The horse is being worked on the circle from predominantly inside aids, with his right side neglected. The result is that the horse hangs on to the inside rein, instead of working and supporting with an active inside hind leg. This rider has lost the essential part of the bending mechanism, when the horse stretches forward through the outside shoulder into the rein on that side. When this horse is asked for smaller circles and the beginnings of exercises which depend upon correct bend and shoulder control, the groundwork will be missing and the evasions will begin.

Correction If you resemble the second rider, you should take the following corrective measures, regardless of your horse's particular abilities or problems:

1. Remain central in the saddle, particularly when difficulties arise.
2. Have control over the position of

Fig 3 The Ditton showing a well-established left bend and working well into the outside rein.

each hand, and the weight in each rein.
3. Have a supple control of both legs so that you can alter the amount and position of the aid without detriment to the seat and upper body position.
4. Make all of these points second nature so that you can simultaneously listen to advice, prepare for the next piece of work or movement, ride amidst others without disturbing their work, remember a test and think forward to areas which will require clever preparation.

These may appear very demanding requirements if you have only recently become interested in schooling your horse more seriously. However, remember that whether you are attempting your first novice test shortly or competing in an Advanced Medium Championship Qualifier class, riding, training and competing at all levels require that you have mastered the 'base': a secure, supple and central posture from which to begin. Don't forget – without it the dancer, the skater and the gymnast would all fall over!

Improving Your Riding

Tuition

In order to make any assessment of your riding and to assist your progress, it is essential that you have some help from the ground. Whether that help is from a riding school where you join an 'own horse' lesson, or from an experienced and successful competition rider who also teaches others, will depend on your

Fig 4 Falcon working in canter with the rider in the centre of the saddle and in a position to control both sides of the horse efficiently.

situation, your finances and, of course, your own choice. If you already work in a group and feel that you benefit from it, then you have probably found an enthusiastic teacher who is capable of helping everyone in the group. Many riders, however, favour small groups or individual tuition.

As a teacher, I find it is frustrating to have a situation where one or two riders in a small group would greatly benefit from seeing me ride their horses and explaining a point while demonstrating it, but riders miss out on this special assistance, due to lack of time. In an individual lesson, there is time for the rider to work under the watchful eye of the trainer, and to see the trainer ride some of the work where there is a problem or new ground to cover. How frequent your visits to your trainer can be usually depends on your finances. Regular attendance is certainly advisable if there are bad habits to correct or difficulties in your horse's way of going.

The work you can do at home will depend upon your facilities, especially during the restrictions imposed by winter weather.

Visual Aids

Be sure that you fully understand the corrections of position which your trainer explains to you. If your lessons take place in a school where there are mirrors, this will help enormously. For example, to see as you approach a mirror

Fig 5 The rider rising to the trot during the first few minutes of the lunge lesson.

that your horse is not quite straight, and to observe yourself making the correction, shows you the degree of correction to associate with the feel of what you did.

Another interesting visual aid to your home corrections is to watch your own shadow when the sun shines on your arena, or on the road if you are out hacking. This can tell you very clearly if you are leaning sideways.

A video recording is definitely the best method of discovering how you sit. It shows all angles and illustrates your problems clearly. Frequently you may think you are dealing with these in a productive way, only to see with your own eyes that you were undoubtedly opposing the line of correction. As with the mirror, it tells you the degree of correction to aim for, but unlike the mirror you can spend as much time as you like in your fireside chair, analysing and learning.

Remember that an untrained eye can often be an observant critic and adviser. I have frequently been amazed by helpers who, when asked to comment, have remarked 'Well I don't know what I'm talking about, but he did seem to carry his bottom to one side a great deal.'

Working on the Lunge

My suggestions so far have been geared towards self-improvement with your own horse. Work and lessons on a well-schooled horse can be of unequalled value, if your riding tuition and training

Fig 6 Most of the work for a fit rider will be without stirrups, to achieve depth of seat and a supple lower back. The rider has a very light hold of the pommel with the outside hand.

Fig 7 A trained horse with a well-balanced canter has no difficulty in giving the rider the benefit of canter work without the stirrups. There is a danger that the seat slips to the outside of the saddle in this situation, so the rider must keep the inside leg stretching down and close to the horse.

is limited to one horse. The best situation in which to have your first experience of a trained horse – and by this I mean a medium level plus horse – is definitely on the lunge.

You will appreciate the need for your lunge horse to be trained to at least medium level the moment he moves off from the halt. This standard of horse will move with more power in his steps than you may previously have experienced. His back will swing in his trot and he should also be capable of giving you the working and collected canter on the lunge quite effortlessly. When I am teaching riders about to mount a trained horse for the first time, we watch the horse being worked in before the lunge lesson. This work will follow the horse's usual loosening up routine. If he is an older horse, this will always include stretching him forward and down in trot and canter, with his rider off his back. Thus, the apprehensive pupil gets to know the horse a little before mounting. He also learns about the rhythm in which the horse will be working. I have the opportunity to tell the pupil about the horse's character and his competitive achievements, so that he has some background information.

When the pupil mounts up, we adjust the stirrups to what he feels is normal. I check that he is not over-ambitious at this stage for a long leg, if I know that his own horse has a less powerful stride. The lesson progresses slowly; beginning with easy trot work with stirrups and reins on each rein. This early trot will be rising, to ease any stiffness in the rider. It is also possible to check the position whilst rising, where there can be a multitude of sins! This is followed by sitting to the working trot, with the reins in both hands, including transitions to and from the walk.

As the rider gains the feel of the rhythm and stride, and balance improves, work without the stirrups, but probably with a light hold of the pommel, can commence. If the horse has an easy, rounded canter on the lunge, then it is an excellent loosening exercise for the rider to shake himself down into the saddle at the canter pace. Obviously all of this work is interspersed with rest periods in walk, and the rider usually takes back his stirrups towards the final quarter of his lesson. How long he works without the stirrups will be determined by his own riding fitness and by how he copes with the bigger, trained paces. The duration of the lesson is generally dictated by the rider's fitness; a minimum of thirty minutes and a maximum of about fifty, for a fit rider, is the average.

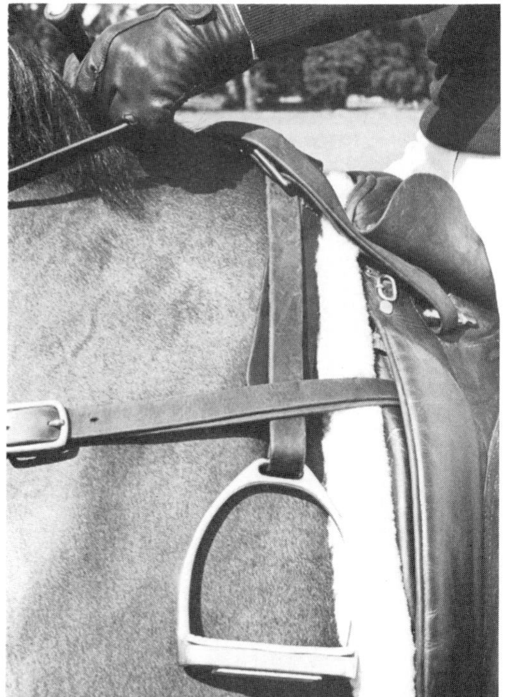

Fig 8 The stirrup leather is laid flat under the skirt of the saddle and the irons must be placed under the side reins so that no weight is put on to the side reins.

The fitter and more experienced rider can take full advantage of the trained horse. Work on small circles; sideways steps towards a larger circle, combined with shortening and lengthening of the stride, can give the rider the chance to improve his aids and have a wider range of work to sit to. Acute transitions, such as from walk to canter and back again, can be perfected without the reins so that the rider appreciates how much can be achieved by good posture, preparation and timing.

To gain full value from lunge lessons, take a series of as many sessions as you can afford. Three or four lunges on consecutive days, topped with a few once-weekly sessions, will give you a great start if you are riding at novice or elementary level. If you are already competing higher up the scale, lunging will tune up your position and aids, and get you deeper in the saddle, especially if you work through the variations within the paces.

The horse and rider should spend some minutes relaxing at the end of the lesson off the lunge line, walking on a long rein. At this stage the rider can review the lesson, considering the areas of work where extra thought is needed for position or aids, and reflecting on the progress which has been achieved.

Fig 9 Working well together in the trot, in readiness for some transitions within the pace to collected and medium trot.

Fig 10 Walking home Caruso stretches his topline in free walk.

Planning for Work

Your Life-style

Where and when you school your horse is inevitably governed by your own life-style, and usually by where you keep the horse and the facilities available. Very few riders are lucky enough to have all year round facilities which enable their training programme to progress with chosen rest periods. If your training year is curtailed by conditions underfoot and lack of daylight in the winter months, draw up a plan of action which works around those restrictions. Give your horse his annual holiday at these times. Make sure immunisation injections, and any other special treatment which requires him to rest from work for a week or so, are also slotted into these enforced breaks.

You could consider the advantages of joining forces with other riders and travelling to an indoor school for an evening's work, when roads are passable but fields and outdoor arenas are frozen solid. However slowly you work, due to woolly coats and lack of fitness, the benefits are twofold. Firstly, you gain practice in boxing up and the opportunity of working in different surroundings. Secondly, you can maintain a low level of fitness with work demanding bends, changes of direction and canter, which road work denies. This fitness provides a substantial base on which you can build up the work more quickly, when conditions permit.

Responsibilities

As a rider it is your responsibility to understand the following:

1. Your horse's temperament, at work and in his stable.
2. Your horse's conformational assets and defects.
3. The requirements of the work at each level of training.
4. The FEI (Federation Equestre Internationale) definitions of movements, especially those at a higher level than your present ability.
5. When your horse has evaded the work asked of him because he is tired, confused or finding the work difficult due to stiffness or conformational restrictions.
6. When to stop! If your horse has worked hard and well, don't force him to repeat everything 'one more time'.

Arena Technique

There is no excuse for the rider who describes circles which resemble eggs and asks for impossible changes of direction because he is looking down. If you lack an arena or fenced-in area, schooling can be more difficult but it is not out of the question. Use cones or old car tyres to mark out the sizes of circles. Poles can be put down too, to create corners and straight lines. Move your props regularly to different areas of your field to avoid poaching the ground and to vary your arena. Your working-in can be away from this area but you must still pay attention to the direction of your lines and the shape and size of your circles.

Setting Your Goals

All riders, whatever the level of their achievement, should set themselves clear goals. The rider who wishes to improve his horse's general versatility and his own

Fig 11 Aim high! Sandy Pleuger Clarke with Marco Polo.

riding ability will set his goals within these boundaries. That rider may not have a competitive streak, so his ambitions will be attained through his own enjoyment and recognition of his horse's progress.

The serious competitor often commences with novice level tests and limited ambitions. If his training is thoughtful and consistent, his horse will improve so much that medium level begins to be a realistic target. Many horses have surprised their riders still more by climbing the ladder right up to Prix St Georges. In doing so, they have provided their riders with an incalculable wealth of experience in both thorough training and competition. The learning then goes full circle if these well-trained horses become schoolmasters for riders who want to gain experience of work at medium level plus, and of flying changes in particular.

In short, you should aim high. Horses can be great levellers, but you may find that yours is full of surprises!

2 Choosing Your Dressage Horse

Selection Factors

Looking for a suitable horse is a difficult task and not always an enjoyable experience. Unless you methodically compile a list of things you do want in a dressage horse and another of what is not acceptable, you will waste much of your own time and that of other people.

The first detail to decide is your price limit, because when you start to make enquiries to buy, no one can help you if you are unsure of your finances. After deciding your price limit, you can draw up your first list, which will consist of things you cannot accept in a dressage horse.

Unacceptable Characteristics

Start the list by putting down all your personal dislikes – any types, colours or markings which are your pet hates.

After this, you can get down to basics. If you are intending to pursue your interest in dressage seriously, the following points should go down on your list of things to avoid.

1. Poor movement Avoid a horse with significant deviation from being straight in his movement in front and behind.

2. Faulty conformation A horse who is built downhill stands naturally higher at his croup. His neck may also be 'set on' low, so that his conformation gives the impression of being loaded in front and on his forehand.

A horse with a badly set on head or neck will give you a lot of trouble. Badly set on means that the natural angle under the jaw-line is so great or 'open' that the horse will have difficulty working through into a rounded outline. If he is very thick in the jowl to neck region the same problem arises. The neck to shoulder connection, as in the case of the croup high horse, is important, and the problem is not easily overcome, if at all.

A very young horse of two, three or even four years old may be standing croup high because he still has some growing to do. Some breeds in particular, and some lines of certain breeds, are known to be late developers. Follow your adviser's opinion on this point, not the vendor's.

3. Wide frame A horse who is very wide through his chest, shoulders and rib-cage will prevent you from riding with the same depth of seat and length of leg as you expect under normal circumstances. From the training angle, the horse may move with a rather rolling action, particularly in the walk.

4. Narrow frame A horse with a narrow frame may have an action which is 'close' in front or behind, or both. If a weak horse who is young or in poor condition brushes, and marks or injures his fetlocks, we can hope that with a steady work programme his movement will become stronger and consequently straighter. However, on this matter, you should seek good veterinary advice – and take it!

5. Awkward stance A horse who stands with his hind legs out behind him will have a lot to do to bring them well under his body in his work. A good rider can assist a horse who is fighting against the odds, but he can only build muscle, not change the framework.

6. Stable tricks and vices Many professionals do not mind a horse who weaves a little if they can keep him out of sight of other horses. On many yards, however, the weaver or crib-biter is not welcome, and rightly so, as horses, like children, do tend to copy the bad habits rather than emulate the good.

However, vices, as they are termed, reduce the value of the horse. If he is a Grand Prix horse and has proved his worth, they hardly matter. If he is five years old and yet to prove himself, vices may mean that although he is a much cheaper horse, he is a questionable investment. If you can deal with the bad habits there is the possibility of acquiring a horse who would otherwise be out of your price range, but who has great talent and potential. However, approach this area with caution.

7. Difficult temperament From the purchasing aspect, it is tempting to buy a handsome thoroughbred who has come out of training because he didn't want to race or wasn't fast enough. Such horses can make the grade in dressage and there are many to prove it. If you find a thoroughbred with a solid temperament, I am sure that he will be an exciting horse to train, with endless stores of energy. However, you need experience and a lot of patience to train such a horse. Don't be tempted unless you can work under the watchful eye of a good teacher on a regular basis. Most importantly, remember to expect slow progress when training.

Desirable Qualities

Having decided what you want to avoid, you can move on to the important list of desirable qualities.

1. Good conformation Look at the horse's frame whilst he is standing normally and also the picture he creates when moving. As you look, imagine the frame of a Grand Prix dressage horse, with the croup lowered and the horse 'coming up' through his back and withers with light, mobile shoulders. The potential for this quality of 'growing up' in front of you should be there in the young horse. You can teach him how to work through his back, by stretching his neck and head down, but he should not be built this way. His natural frame should remind you of that Grand Prix outline, not a working down outline.

Look at the whole horse for strength, If there is a slight weakness, is it balanced out by a strong point? The hind leg must show the potential to push with a big, clean hock, to help carry the weight in collection and extension.

The feet in every hard-working horse must be sound and healthy. If your horse reaches advanced level, he will be treated to all-weather surfaces for his compet-

Fig 12 When looking for the ideal horse, imagine the frame of a Grand Prix horse. Could he have a lowered croup and light mobile shoulders in four years time? Jane Bartle Wilson with Pinnochio.

ition work. On his way up the ladder, through novice and elementary at least, he will have to work on some very hard arenas. He must be sound as he has a lot of work ahead.

2. A horse to suit your life-style You must consider how your domestic or work commitments will influence your choice of horse. Will he live partially out? Will he be ridden every day?

If he is in the care of a good livery yard, and his work and hacking are daily, then you can choose a horse who needs and thrives on work. His height and type of conformation must suit you, and you must feel and look right for each other. The idea that you need a fairly big horse to attract attention is not true. A horse at 15.2hh., who has plenty of presence, will fill the eye with his way of going and his character will shine through.

The choice of a particular breed is up to you. There are plenty of horses available by good English thoroughbreds, while a three-quarter bred with some native blood such as Welsh Cob can prove to be a very versatile horse and a good mover.

3. A horse to match your ambitions Have you thought seriously about how far up the dressage ladder you wish to climb? I predict that you will become more addicted if, at present, you are on the bottom rung of the ladder. You should look at each horse which you consider with your ambitions in mind. Will he cope with medium level work and can you picture flying changes from his canter? I am, of course, not suggesting that you consider a horse who is beyond your capabilities right now, because that never works, but he must show enough of the desirable qualities which you have listed.

4. Temperament A calm and consistent temperament, compatible with your own will make training and competing enjoyable and usually more rewarding. Calm and consistent does not mean dull or mechanical. We all enjoy owning a horse who is full of character, and when the mixture of desirable attributes is right the result can be a sparkling, entertaining and obedient horse. A horse who shows brilliance but is unreliable on the big occasion is a nightmare to own. He cannot be trusted, and trust is essential if your partnership is to have a sound base.

5. Good paces and way of going The walk is important and when you watch a horse walking on a loose rein, the steps he makes should be long and even in length. There should be no impression of tension, nor any inclination to hurry out of the rhythm.

If there is a problem in the walk, it will show itself when you take up the reins and ask for medium walk with a positive contact. A clever and experienced rider can improve walk problems through good riding and by making the horse supple through all his paces, but if you are choosing a horse of seven years old or more, beware of any frequent evidence of a 'choppy', hurried walk. Similarly, avoid

Fig 13 The Ditton in free walk.

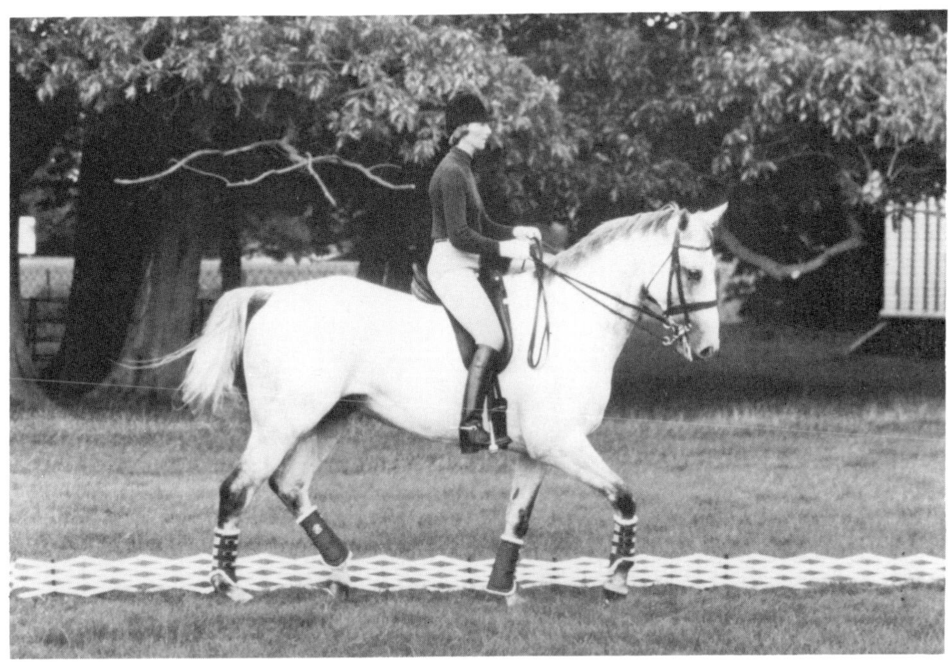

Fig 14 The Ditton shortening his trot whilst maintaining impulsion.

Fig 15 The Ditton with his medium trot giving the impression that he has an equal ability to shorten and to lengthen his stride.

a horse whose steps look uneven in length, particularly behind, due to stiffness of the back and excitable temperament.

A horse who is unhappy in his mouth will, through hollowing away from the bit, show a poor walk, lacking in length of stride and rhythm. Do not be afraid to spend plenty of time observing the horse's walk, as it is always revealing and informative.

Your considerations concerning the trot should be twofold: the length of the stride, and the horse's manner of working, through his entire body, in the pace. When you observe the stride in the working trot, ask yourself whether the horse shows an equal ability to shorten or lengthen his working trot. If his stride is impressively long, ask yourself whether his frame will lend itself to collection. If his stride is short, with just a little too much knee action, consider whether his shoulders are capable of opening up more, and whether he can work with a softer back. The way the horse works through his back influences the length of his stride. He should swing through his topline, and his tail must move accordingly.

A slightly restricted trot, in which the horse has a reasonable stride but has not been encouraged to swing and use himself enough, can often be improved dramatically. If the walk and the canter are unspoilt and promising, a trot which is below par can be well ridden to bring it up to the standard of other paces.

The criteria for assessing the working canter are similar to those for the trot. Consider whether you can shorten or lengthen the stride a little, with equal potential, even in the younger horse. This is a simple yardstick.

The canter must give a feeling of balance and lightness. If the horse is being pushed too fast in the pace, especially when he is young, then this will unbalance him. If the general feeling is promising and the three-time beat is clear and true, then any slight crookedness and loss of balance caused by inadequate riding can be repaired and the pace improved. If the horse is very crooked, through stiffness and habit, particularly on one rein, then you will have to take into account his age when you make your decision.

Whereas a mediocre trot can be vastly improved through a good canter pace, the opposite does not apply. Significant loosening and improvement of the trot can be produced from a clever pattern of work with a good rider. I have seen horses of ten and eleven years old improve dramatically when an experienced rider has taken them on for a period of a few months. These are exceptions; generally speaking if a horse is stiff and 'set' in his back at eight or nine years old, it will be an uphill struggle to change him.

These are general guidelines, and you may wish to add some requirements of your own, gleaned from experiences with horses which you have previously owned or ridden.

The Search for a Horse

There are several possible ways of finding information about horses for sale: magazines, newspapers and agencies; by word of mouth – in your riding club, and at competitions; by contacting a reputable dealer; by contacting dressage trainers who may have pupils with well-recommended horses to sell.

Whichever avenue you follow, when you reach the telephoning stage there are vital questions which may save you a large telephone bill, at least, and a long wasted journey later. Ask these questions early in your conversation:

1. What is the price? Is the vendor open to offers?
2. Will the vendor allow vetting, and possibly X-rays of front feet or joints?
3. Does the horse have any large blemishes or particular lumps and bumps? Does he move straight?
4. Does the vendor warrant him sound and free from undesirable stable habits and vices such as crib-biting, windsucking and weaving?
5. Is the horse good to box up? How does he behave in traffic and away from his home?

From here you have to go into the intricacies of why he is for sale, his history, and also raise any of your own particular queries.

Going to Try the Horse

There are some golden rules to observe when trying a horse. If you are viewing during the winter months, ascertain that there will be facilities for you to do all the trials which are necessary. You cannot try out his ability to lengthen his stride on a rutty, rock-hard hillside. If it is necessary to box the horse up and travel him to a centre with an all-weather arena, then this must be worth it, to buyers, vendor and horse alike.

If you know that you wish to see him jump then you must verify that this will be possible. Give prior warning if you wish to ride out in traffic; the present owner has every right to stipulate that this part of the trial is subject to him assessing your riding ability first. He will doubtless want to organise an escort to accompany you on the ride out.

If all your questions were answered favourably in your initial enquiries, take your trainer or adviser with you on the first visit. See the horse in his stable at rest. If possible, see him with just his bridle on, standing out on the yard where you can freely move around him and get a clear picture of his overall outlook and conformation.

Find a flat stretch of hard ground – but not gravel – to see him walked to and fro, and trotted boldly out. It is useful to observe him again in the stable, being saddled up ready to be worked.

See the horse's own rider work him first. Don't be frightened to ask the rider to walk him about his field or arena for a few minutes, on a long rein, when he leaves the yard. It is a valuable occasion for watching his general attitude and reactions. Depending upon the horse's fitness, either you or your trainer should then have a 'sit on'. If he is not very fit or strong, then you, the potential rider, ought to get the feel of his paces before he tires. Your adviser may then check on any doubtful points which you may have noticed.

There will be many other questions to ask and useful observations to discuss. When you have done all this you will know either that you really don't like the horse enough, or that he seems to be exactly what you require. If the first of these is the case, tell the owner that you don't wish to buy and thank him for his time and trouble. If you like the horse, say so! You may wish to mull over your eventual decision on the journey home, but personally I never find this useful. If it is necessary to go away and rethink, there must be some reasonable doubts in your mind, in which case, leave the horse behind.

If you decide to purchase the horse, brief the veterinary surgeon whom you ask to examine him regarding your findings and the exact future training and activities which you would like the horse to take on. Whether to X-ray or not is debatable, but it is the buyer's decision, and is required by some insurance companies, so it is wise to do your homework on this subject. It is usual for the veterinary surgeon to discuss his findings with you in some detail; he gives his opinion, you must make your decision.

Assessing Your Present Horse

If you already have a good horse in the stable, assess him thoroughly. Check through the lists of things to avoid and desirable qualities. Tick off your horse's good points first. What are his special qualities? Are you making the most of them? Then consider his faults, such as any awkwardness in his way of going. From your answers, you may find yourself going back to the drawing board for a few weeks to revise some of the basics.

Don't forget the value of recording your work on video, as this may reveal some areas of your work with which you are so familiar that you have become complacent. If there are long-standing bad habits which you find difficult to change, invest in some lessons on a trained horse. You will find that this will recharge your batteries and give you some new objectives. It is important to have goals, both in training itself and in the competitive scene. Make a training plan.

Competition Prospects

Dressage horses come in a variety of shapes and sizes. However, any horse can be trained to medium level, provided that he has not had too many years of indifferent performance and become a very stiff late starter. Prix St Georges is within the reach of most horses and riders, so whether you are buying a new horse or reassessing and improving your present partner, you should set your sights on this level. The trot work at this level is within reach, and the canter must have the lift, suppleness and co-ordination to change and link the sequence changes together. The stiffer horse, however, might be caught out by the demi pirouette in the canter.

The two levels of intermediate and the top rung of Grand Prix can be reached by a horse of sound structure with three good paces. He must have consistent, progressive training to build muscles which produce the power for demanding movements such as *Piaffe* and *Passage*, canter pirouettes and one time changes. This training takes at least four years, after which more years of consolidation are required in working for perfection.

Portraits

The ideal dressage horse has a strong frame with no serious weakness, a generous temperament, and the will to work as a partner. His shape and size can be surprisingly varied, as you will see from the following portraits. These brief histories of individual horses will illustrate possible breeds, types and characteristics to suit different enthusiasts and their way of life.

Daylight Monarch (Figs 16 & 17)

Age and height 12 years old, 16.0hh.

Breeding Seven-eighths thoroughbred
Sire: Armagnac Monarch
Dam: Irish bred out of a pony mare by Middle Temple

Type Elegant and lightweight but with substance.

Credentials Working hunter champion; successful in intermediate horse trials, hunter trials and affiliated dressage, up to and including medium level.

Temperament Very kind and easy going.

Work quota He needs plenty of fast work to keep him fit and sparkling as his temperament leads to a complacent attitude to life.

Owner Air stewardess, so 'Bugsy' is kept at livery. Owner does the serious training when at home. The livery yard rides him to keep him on his toes in between.

Conclusions The rider needs a reliable back-up team. The horse needs fast work and a busy life for a high level of fitness. His temperament accepts happily the irregular serious training and competitive outings with his rider.

Caruso (Figs 18 & 19)

Age and height 19 years old, 16.0hh.

Breeding Swedish warmblood

Type Middleweight within a small frame, so very compact and strong.

Credentials Grand Prix de Dressage winner in his native land. Now a generous schoolmaster for work including one time changes, longreining and lunging.

Temperament Kind and genuine, but very lazy!

Work quota Now requires a daily loosening programme of 'working down'. Short and sharp revision of his advanced work twice a week, hacks and lunge lessons fill up the remainder of his working week.

Owner On loan to me. My team learn from him and keep him fit and busy. He dislikes life in the field, preferring to keep an eye on activities in the yard; an example of an older gentleman who does not wish to be retired.

Conclusions Caruso's work and fitness are his lifeline. A successful ex-competitor who thrives on activity, his loosening exercises are a daily ritual to retain suppleness and muscle tone. He is proof that a horse does not have to be a giant to make it to the top rung. If the vital ingredients are there, and you can train him, a good 'little un' will always make the grade.

Fig 16 Daylight Monarch, 16hh. Twelve years old, seven-eighths thoroughbred. Sire Armagnac Monarch.

Fig 17 Daylight Monarch, working in canter, shows the neat, compact outline of a very adaptable and capable performer.

Fig 18 Caruso, 16hh. Nineteen years old, Swedish by Sorrento out of Cadenza.

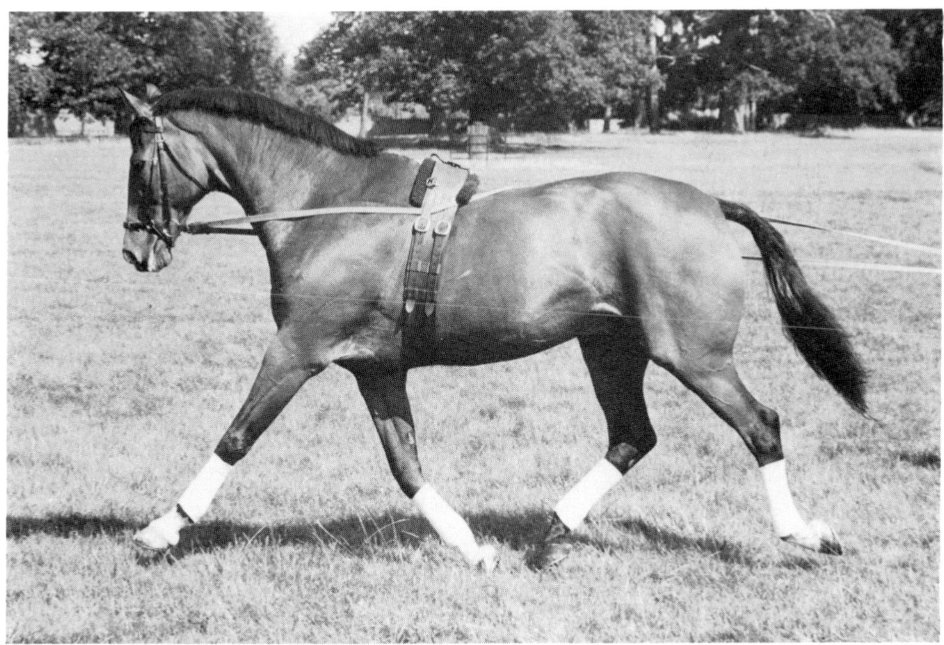

Fig 19 A great ex-competitor, seen here on the long reins.

Duchess (Figs 20 & 21)

Age and height 11 years old, 16.1hh.

Breeding Irish draught
Sire: King of Diamonds

Type Very strong conformation, middleweight.

Credentials A successful Riding Club competitor, including Championship level horse trials and jumping. Competes in Novice and Elementary level dressage tests.

Temperament A chestnut lady with a lot of personality. She has enthusiasm and a genuine attitude towards what she is asked to tackle.

Work quota She has a tendency to hurry through her work and requires slowing down exercises and lots of transitions to walk to establish her best rhythm, first in trot, and later in canter. However, her temperament is such that she does not need a lot of mileage in her everyday work; a hack often precedes her schooling sessions to help her to settle to her work immediately.

Owner Farmer's wife and mother who cares for her own horse at home. Duchess is schooled as regularly as her busy owner's commitments will permit. Her type and temperament make it possible for her to thrive on work, but she still remains kind and co-operative to ride if she has missed a few days' exercise. The horse's ability, coupled with some difficulties in maintaining outline and rhythm, encourage the owner to school her and work to a plan on the days available.

Conclusions Duchess is 'safe', to suit an owner with family responsibilities and variable time availability. She is also enthusiastic and so provides her owner with good competition outings. Although 'safe', she is not 'easy', and she therefore provides a challenge, on a regular basis, for her rider.

The Ditton (Figs 22 & 23)

Age and height 9 years old, 16.3hh.

Breeding Sire: The Ditton
Dam: three-quarter-bred hunter mare

Type Big, rangy horse of three-day event type.

Credentials Early education and competitive work was of a comprehensive nature – dressage, cross country, combined training. From six years old his training and competing have been through levels of dressage. At nine years old, his present level of advanced medium work has fallen behind schedule by a year or more, due to delays caused by an accident.

Temperament Basically kind and very sensitive, yet clever and strong-willed. He needs plenty of time to relax alone in his field if he is to work calmly.

Work quota Clever horses always require plenty of work, but often they need persuading of this fact! Ditton leads an active life. He works in the school for four or five days a week and hacks out in the countryside on the remaining days. He spends very little time in his stable as he is not happy without his daily quota of hours in the field. If he is short changed,

Fig 20 Duchess, 16.1hh. Eleven years old, Irish Draught mare by King of Diamonds.

Fig 21 Duchess in working trot. I am working rising to encourage her back to swing and to create roundness of outline.

Fig 22 The Ditton, 16.3hh. Nine years old, by The Ditton. Three-quarters thoroughbred.

Fig 23 Bred to event but showing the ability to perform well on the flat.

he will not let himself be caught!

Owner Owned by myself. Due to my busy life he is ridden equally often by my assistant. He is a demanding horse who requires a great deal of attention from the few people he respects. Complete days off occur only after competition outings, so he requires attention on a full-time basis.

Conclusions Ditton is not every rider's cup of tea, but if you have complete faith in a horse who gives you the most exciting rides, you find yourself prepared to go to any lengths in the attempt to take him to the top.

William (Figs 24 & 25)

Age and height 7 years old, 17.0hh.

Breeding Sire: Irish Trill
Dam: Hunter mare

Type A strong horse who bears a rider's weight easily, but is not heavyweight in stature or way of carrying himself.

Credentials Has hunted and been a good novice all-rounder for a tall gentleman owner who required a big, but not heavy, horse. Schooled on the flat to elementary level by lightweight ladies, for their education and his.

Temperament Kind and genuine. An inquisitive horse who can have difficulty in concentrating on his work.

Work quota An interesting horse who can adapt to suit an experienced rider when he is fit, yet kind enough to help a novice rider in a less demanding situation. His working programme is based on regularity, for as with any big horse he requires a certain level of fitness to remain healthy. The quantity of work could be as little as half an hour road exercise plus half an hour schooling a day, but without missing many days.

Owner Because William would not be suited to living mostly out, due to his waistline, he is placed at livery. Due to his kind temperament he can fill a dual-purpose role, providing his businessman owner with enjoyable training rides at weekends, and those who school him with challenges which are rewarding when they get it right.

Conclusions A rare type of horse who, although not a schoolmaster, can adapt. A back-up team is necessary because he needs a level of fitness maintained. Able to work well in his schooling sessions, with the potential to go to medium level plus.

Crimson Pennant (Figs 26 & 27)

Age and height 13 years old, 16.0hh.

Breeding Sire: Don Carlos
Dam: Thoroughbred

Type Well-muscled thoroughbred. Excellent conformation based on a strong frame.

Credentials In training and raced until six years old, followed by a short spell of jumping education. From seven years old owned and trained by a dressage enthusiast. Working at Prix St George level and enjoys his work.

Fig 24 William, 17hh. Seven years old, by Irish Trill. Middleweight gelding.

Fig 25 William was bred to hunt but is capable of being trained to medium level.

Fig 26 Crimson Pennant, 16hh. Thirteen years old, thoroughbred ex-racehorse by Don Carlos.

Fig 27 Working trot showing a well-muscled up frame after six years of hard work. A naturally compact, athletic horse.

Temperament Kind, sometimes unreliable, but not hot-tempered. Improving steadily, even at this age.

Work quota Thrives on his work and learns easily. His daily work pattern includes schooling and working through his repertoire for about half an hour each day. This is followed by walking out in very hilly countryside – hence his amazing muscles. As a young horse just out of training, he needed a fair amount of mileage but as the regular, calming work began to steady his temperament, vast quantities of work were no longer needed.

Owner Owner gained mileage and experience on a variety of horses before she took on this one. He is stabled at home and his owner rides and takes care of him single-handed. He has his daily routine of early morning work and exercise, followed by time in the field later in the day.

Conclusions Pennant is now secure in his routine work. He swapped careers at quite a late stage in life, and only thanks to a very patient and determined owner-rider has he adjusted and begun to enjoy working at a high level in dressage. He took time to settle with his new owner and a different type of outing in his horse box.

If you are considering a horse who has raced, remember that you may have some very exciting first outings (hopefully non-competitive) when he imagines he is racing again. The thoroughbred can work well at dressage, but he must have a rider who understands him and is not in a hurry.

Limited Edition (Figs 28 & 29)

Age and height 5 years old, 16.1hh.

Breeding Part-bred Arab
Sire: Master Cast (Anglo Arab)
Dam: Hunter mare

Type Lightweight, good frame and limbs.

Credentials Backed and ridden in spring of her fourth year. Taken out and about to gain experience. Learning to jump and commencing preliminary and novice dressage competitions at present.

Temperament 'Bee Bee' is very calm and accepts new situations, enjoying outings and activity.

Work quota Most of her work at this stage is sensible hacking. It is difficult to prevent her from becoming too fit, therefore she spends a great deal of her time in her field, and is schooled only once or twice a week. The schooling includes a weekly jumping lesson of grid work.

Owner The owner bred Bee Bee, so she is totally home-grown and cared for. In better weather they ride out in the early mornings and once a week they box up and go to good hacking country to keep up the horse's interest. Regular lessons ensure that she progresses in schooling. Because she is not encouraged to become too fit, she remains a manageable, bright young horse. When the winter weather strikes, the horse is tough enough to be out during the day. Her temperament allows her to miss a few days' riding and remain 'safe' for her owner to mount her again.

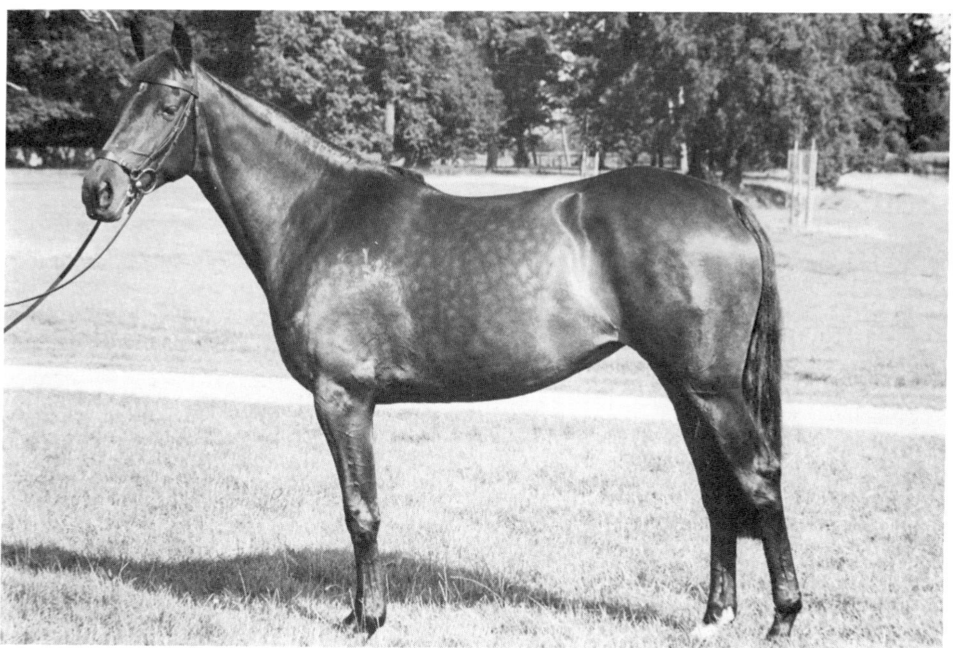

Fig 28 Limited Edition, 16.1hh. Five years old, part bred Arab mare by Master Cast.

Fig 29 A neat mare who moves well, with potential to work on the flat and over fences.

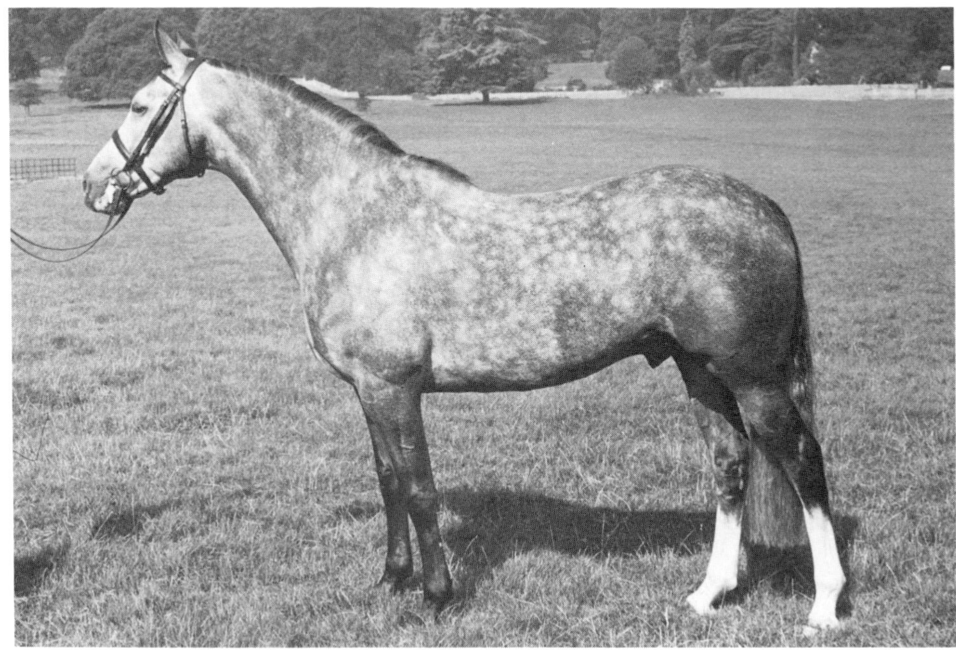

Fig 30 Bushbaby, 15.2hh. Seven years old, by Hill Farmer out of a Welsh cob cross thoroughbred.

Fig 31 Bred for a Welsh farmer to hunt but definitely a serious dressage contender with good paces.

Conclusions I would not encourage a busy owner-rider of novice level to go out and buy this type of horse. We have moulded Bee Bee's lifestyle so that she is suitable for her breeder-owner to enjoy and learn on safely. Safety must be a prime factor when a rider goes out and about alone on the horse.

Bushbaby (Figs 30 & 31)

Age and height 7 years old, 15.2hh.

Breeding Three-quarter thoroughbred one-quarter Welsh cob.

Type Very strong and compact, with a big frame for his height.

Credentials Remained entire until four years old. Cheeky to back and begin training. His early work was geared towards jumping. From five years old his main interest has been dressage and he learns well. He is now working at medium level and consolidating his changes, which he often did naturally when feeling fresh as a youngster.

Temperament Kind, but reacts very sharply and has a suspicious streak. He enjoys a busy life, and showing off.

Work quota Schools hard approximately four days each week. The other days are spent hacking, with a strong canter for fun, and doing some jumping, which has always encouraged good flying changes.

Owner His rider is with him every day, and is in the ideal situation of knowing her horse well, both in and out of the stable. He is worked with fitness and progress in mind. When the rider has a day off, he has a day in the field. Their commitment to each other works well.

Conclusions Horse and rider are fully committed to serious training. They have the time, and they both want to enjoy their learning and competing.

Ping Pong (Figs 32 & 33)

Age and height 7 years old, 16.3hh.

Breeding Danish – details unknown.

Type Strong thoroughbred type, lightweight but robust.

Credentials Hunted hard in Leicestershire from four to six years old. A latecomer to dressage, she has a mind of her own, and is also learning to slow down her jumping and improve her style over fences.

Temperament Strong and bold. Can work obediently, but needs a great variety of work to keep her quick mind occupied.

Work quota Daily roadwork or schooling. She needs the regular activity, but since she easily maintains her natural fitness, she needs time in her field to relax and attempt to become fatter rather than fitter. While she is learning she needs some slower mileage; the speed can wait until she tackles some events.

Owner Ping Pong's rider has a long working day in the City. She has some help with the midweek road walking in the winter months, but does most of the schooling and homework herself. There

Fig 32 Ping Pong, 16.3hh. Seven years old, Danish bred mare.

Fig 33 Having hunted fast and hard in Leicestershire, forward seat work is a necessary tactic at present. The paces and frame are very promising.

Fig 34 The Dark Falcon, 16.3hh. Ten years old, thoroughbred by Conwyn out of Castle Belle.

Fig 35 Bred to race but was a late developer. A generous temperament and well-proportioned frame have adapted well to make him trainable to Grand Prix dressage level.

can be no set timing for this, so Ping Pong has learned to adapt to peculiar routines. She accepts boxing up in the early morning or late evening for a lesson in an indoor school where some dressage or athletic jumping can be done.

Conclusions Horses do learn to adapt, and sometimes riders worry about unusual routines needlessly. With winter competitions becoming more popular, it is commonplace for a horse to be expected to perform a test, or jump a course, at 10.30 p.m., so Ping Pong's practice now may pay off in the future.

The Dark Falcon (Figs 34 & 35)

Age and height 10 years old, 16.3hh.

Breeding Thoroughbred
Sire: Conwyn
Dam: Castle Belle

Type Lightweight but with a big top line. Entire until four years old, so quite cresty.

Credentials Show winner as a young horse, including hunter classes. Specialised in dressage from six years onwards. Trained to intermediate II level. He is an enjoyable horse and schoolmaster.

Temperament Genuine and bold. He can be cheeky when in hand, but is calm and receptive to training and very easy to teach.

Work quota Works daily, with four or five days' schooling a week and hacks in between. He enjoys some jumping for fun and variety, and sometimes plays the part of schoolmaster to help riders on and off the lunge.

Owner My own horse. We enjoy our work sessions together, keeping each other tuned up and working at a high level. We are not able to work together daily, so the back-up team is essential for a horse at this level. He must be kept supple daily, even though it is not necessary for him to perform difficult and demanding movements every day.

Conclusions Rather like owning a Rolls Royce! He needs careful tuning on a regular basis. Although Falcon enjoys being in the field three or four times weekly, this is in addition to work which keeps him supple: it cannot replace it. When a horse has been accustomed to daily training in the early stages of his career, it must continue once he has learned the movements, so that he remains fit to perform the work which he has been taught.

3 Fitness

Once you have acquired your horse, you will no doubt be determined to train him well. You will have established how far up the dressage ladder you aim to go, and at which levels you would like to compete. At this point, you must honestly assess whether your riding fitness, and that of your horse, is as good as it could be.

Rider Fitness

Frequently when I am helping riders with their own horses, a rider comes to a halt in need of a moment's break to restore his own energy levels. This happens most often when he is encountering difficulties in maintaining an exercise, or when riding through some movements of a test, which have posed problems. There may be several reasons why this rider finds himself unable to continue working:

1. He may be in very soft condition, with his muscles unable to work well for even short sessions of activity and effort.
2. He may be very stiff and sitting badly, which can also lead to premature tiredness.
3. His breathing may be shallow and hurried, using quick short breaths to take in the amount of oxygen required to supply the body, enabling it to work efficiently. Tension, due to lack of confidence, goes hand in hand with hurried breathing and results in stress on the mind and body.

Assessing Fitness Required

The first point to consider is your own degree of fitness. Can you work your horse through his daily repertoire (not hacking) and still feel fresh afterwards? Can you ride through the final movements of a test in competition and know that you are performing as efficiently and stylishly as you were at the beginning of the test? Even if you have answered these questions in the affirmative, you probably have a nagging suspicion that you could help your horse more, and correct him with quicker reactions if you were fitter.

Stable work and other manual work, with or without horses, is not conducive to good riding posture or fitness for riding. Unfortunately it is excellent for producing large shoulders and aching backs. This means that unless you are lucky enough to ride three or four horses every day, you need to develop the stretching capacity of the muscles which do the work in schooling riding.

In many sports muscle bulk and power is required. This may be in order to throw or kick a ball as far as possible, through power and technique; it may be needed to spring, or to cycle long distances. In dressage this type of muscle building is not required. The weight of the rider's body is carried equally upon both seat-bones. The muscles of the back, abdomen and seat support the body with supple control. The muscles of the thigh and calf need strength to work effectively within a long, stretching down leg, but it is not helpful if these muscles are developed in a way which makes them bulky.

We may conclude from this that stretching exercises are most useful to build and maintain fitness for riding. Daily stretching will bring you considerable relief if you stiffen up easily, particularly after sitting or travelling for long periods. Breathing well, by learning to use the full expansion of the lungs and to control the speed of breathing, can also contribute, at all levels, to riding a thoughtful, panic-free test.

Finding the Time

I often used to make the excuse of having no time to exercise until a friend gave me some simple but sound advice: 'You only have one body; don't abuse it!' It makes sense to exercise every day. If your body tends to be stiff first thing in the morning, choose a time later in the day when you can exercise for twenty minutes without interruption. Once you have established an exercise pattern and you feel an improvement – which you will after only a few days – this will spur you on. Never miss more than one day, as continuity is essential. If you are bored by the very thought of attempting to exercise on your own, play your favourite music.

Exercise

Swimming has to gain top marks as an exercise which works the whole body. Circulatory and pulmonary systems are fully stretched without joints and back being jarred, as is the case with jogging along the road. The problem with swimming is, generally, the amount of time required for travelling to a pool.

Jogging can be useful, with several provisos. If you intend to use the roads or pavements you need suitable trainers. If you have a soft all-weather arena at your disposal, change into your trainers and do ten minutes of twenty-metre circles and changes of rein. Remember that excessive jogging works against the ideal length of leg for stretching down in dressage. The calf muscles, particularly, grow in width, but will refuse to stretch.

If you have a back or hip weakness jogging is out of the question. If you jog, do so for about ten to fifteen minutes and follow it with five minutes of the stretching exercises described later in this chapter.

Cycling can be fun, strengthens legs and does not jar the joints. If you have a racing bicycle with a high saddle position it stretches the whole leg. The disadvantages of this form of exercise are the slightly rounded back and shoulder position which one easily drops into, and the over-developed calf muscle again growing widthways.

Exercising at Home

As with your horse, when you work your own body through a programme of exercise, select exercises which help a particular part of your body whilst working the body as a whole unit. Concentrate on the parts of your body which you see as the weak links in your riding, but take care not to favour them too much in your repertoire of exercises.

Choose loose, easy clothes such as a track suit to work in, and if you are intending to eat a large supper, exercise first! The following exercises are easy to learn and you will quickly feel the benefit where they stretch and loosen you. You may count to three, five or even ten seconds in the 'holding' part of each exercise. Set your own counts and increase them by one or two seconds each day. Breathe in deeply and exhale fully throughout your exercises, so that you begin to notice your breathing. This will train you to use the same technique when you are riding.

Standing Exercises

Rag doll rolls

1. Stand with shoulders relaxed, keeping your body tall and without stiffness.
2. Roll your head full circle 'rag doll' style, three times to the right and three times to the left.

Warning: do not do this exercise whilst mounted, as a sudden movement from your horse can twist or whiplash your neck.

Shoulder shrugs and rotation

1. Shrug your shoulders: hold them up to your ears, drop them naturally and repeat three times.
2. Rotate the right shoulder – forward, up, back and down – three times.
3. Repeat three times with the left shoulder, and then again with the right and again with the left.
4. Now work both shoulders in both directions, concentrating on your breathing.

Waistline worker

1. Stand with your feet about two feet apart, hands lightly on your hips with your thumbs behind. Bend forwards a little and begin a circular movement with the upper body – forward, bend right, backwards, bend left, return to the front – allowing your head and neck to follow naturally.
2. Do a full circle to the left.
3. Repeat the exercise each way, progressing slowly, day by day, to a lower and fuller circle. Do not force the backward bend and keep your shoulders relaxed.

Sideways stretch

1. With your feet two to three feet apart, stretch your arms out to the sides at shoulder level.
2. Bend a little to the left, stretching your right arm over your head, and sliding your left hand down the left leg to rest on the knee. Hold the position and count, starting with three seconds and increasing the hold daily.
3. Slowly return to upright.
4. Repeat the exercise bending right, and hold for the same count.
5. Slowly return to upright, repeating the movements once more each way. Think about your breathing.

Jog on the spot a little, shake your shoulders, arms and legs and move about to keep you loosened up for the floor exercises.

Floor Exercises

Whole body stretch

1. Sitting up, stretch out your arms straight in front at shoulder level, with your legs straight and together.
2. Slowly lower your back to the floor, dropping your chin lightly onto your chest. Take your arms right back and over, with your whole body stretched flat on your back.
3. Now sit up slowly, without lurching suddenly, and continue stretching your arms forward and down with your body.

4. Rest your hands lightly on knees or calves if possible, lifting your elbows and relax your head down.
5. Slowly return to an upright position and begin once more.
6. Repeat the whole exercise three to six times.

Stomach tightening and spine stretching

1. Lie flat on your back, with your arms naturally at your sides, palms down.
2. Raise both legs together slowly and bring them right back over your head as far as you can reach. Toes should touch the floor, with your legs stretching as much as possible.
3. Uncurl your legs slowly down and forward to your starting position.
4. Repeat the whole exercise three to six times.

Sideways leg stretch

1. Lie on your left side, with your legs straight, one on top of the other. Put both hands flat on floor in front of you, with the fingernails touching. Balance yourself on your right hand and on your left forearm and hand.
2. Raise your right leg straight up, away from your left leg, and count to three. Lower your leg and repeat three times.
3. Turn onto your right side and repeat the same upward stretching with your left leg. Repeat three times.

Back and stomach treatment

1. Lie flat on your stomach with your arms at the side, palms up.
2. Raise your chin and right leg straight up, a few inches from ground. Repeat the exercise a little higher with the same leg.
3. Repeat the exercise with your left leg. Allow your forehead to rest on the floor for a few seconds, and then repeat. This is very good for the lower back, but progress slowly.

These eight simple exercises will work your whole body. Remember that however busy your working day is, it will not be toning and stretching your body in the way these exercises will in fifteen to twenty minutes.

Breathing

In order to learn to breathe well, inhale slowly and use the whole of your rib-cage, expanding it fully. Exhale slowly and be conscious of expelling every last puff of air. When you are riding, practise breathing in this way, especially when you are confronted with a problem.

Exercises in the Saddle

It is my belief that the rider has no business to use his horse as some sort of gymnasium to warm up on. Get yourself supple and fit properly with exercise at home, and you will find that the position, the effect and the work which you have been aiming to achieve will be accomplished. However, when you first mount up and are walking out to prepare your horse for work, some loosening away of the thighs and knees is useful. This can be done by lifting both knees slowly out and away from the saddle flap and allowing both legs to drop heavily, and free from tension, on to your horse's sides. Shrugging the shoulders at this time is very relaxing. Then you are ready to begin.

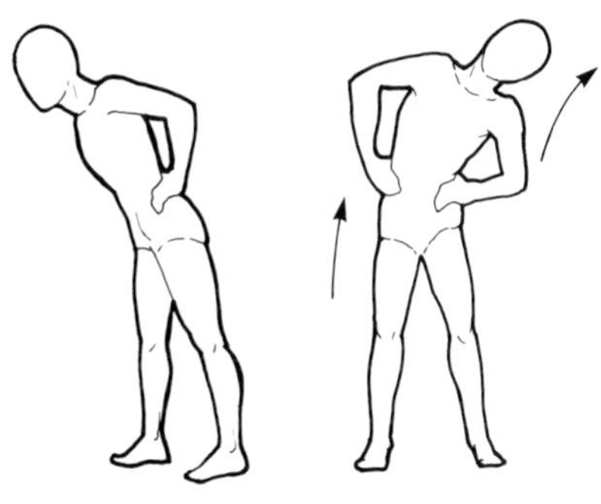
FORWARD BEND
BEGIN ROTATION - SIDEWAYS

Fig 36 Waistline worker.

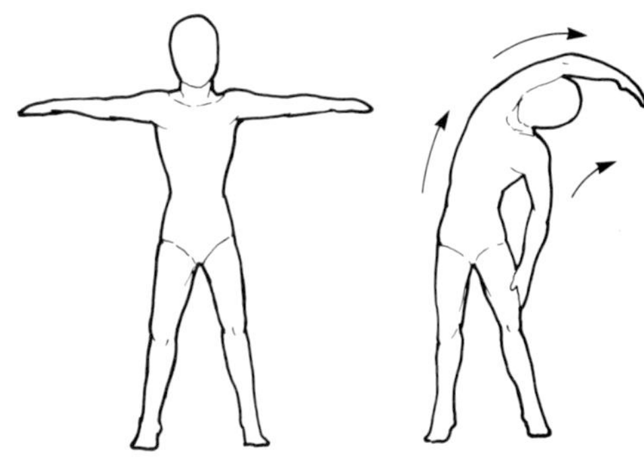
STRETCH TALL ARMS TO SIDE
STRETCH OVER SIDEWAYS DO NOT LEAN FORWARD

Fig 37 Sideways stretch.

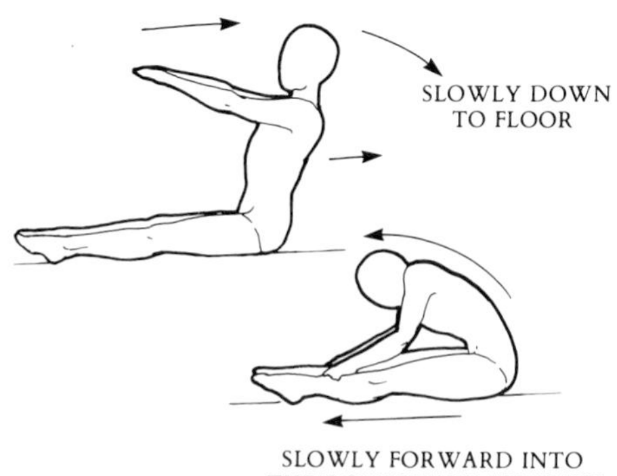
SLOWLY DOWN TO FLOOR
SLOWLY FORWARD INTO THE DOWNWARD STRETCH

Fig 38 Whole body stretch.

Fig 39 Stomach tightening and spine stretching.

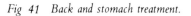

ON YOUR SIDE - ONE FOREARM AND BOTH HANDS BALANCE
RAISE TOP LEG AND HOLD

Fig 40 Sideways leg stretch.

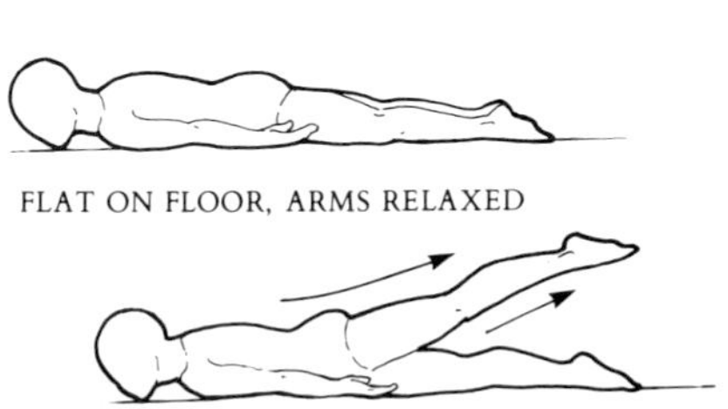
FLAT ON FLOOR, ARMS RELAXED
KEEP BODY FLAT, DO NOT TWIST PELVIS RAISE LEG AND HOLD

Fig 41 Back and stomach treatment.

Your Horse's Fitness

A Grand Prix horse has to be fit to perform the movements of a long and demanding test, with impulsion and control throughout. His ability to produce a good test is founded on his knowledge, his ability to achieve the technical requirements, and the fitness to make them appear effortless and impressive. The suppleness and muscle power which make this possible have been progressively developed over the years, as he has worked through his levels of training. There will have been some breaks in training, due to illness and holidays but by design they will hopefully only have lasted a few days or weeks, not months, risking the loss of muscle tone.

Coming down the ladder a few rungs, the horse working and competing seriously at medium and Prix St Georges level must be fit enough to follow a strenuous work pattern on at least four days a week. The travel and competition which are an integral part of these levels are demanding, sometimes even exhausting. The fitness required to cope with such demands must be considered and worked for with a projected progress and competition plan in mind. This involves several months, not weeks, of training and fittening.

At novice and elementary level your

Fig 42 The Grand Prix horse. Training and development of the muscles to produce an equine athlete of this level takes a minimum of four years, often followed by several years of consolidation.

horse must be fit enough to produce two good tests on a competition day. He should come out for the second test ready to give you an enthusiastic ride, after a shortened working-in period. If he is dull, his fitness may be questionable, and the travelling and standing throughout the day may have taken their toll. A young horse new to competition outings should feel fit enough to enjoy his day, participate in one test and generally learn the ropes. If he is very 'tucked-up' after travelling, then he is not quite ready, is very tense, or your journey has been too long.

There are many books which cover the various aspects of feeding and fittening admirably and in detail. The purpose of this chapter is to collate information which relates to the preparation of horses in early general training and those specialising in dressage. Here is my check-list of priorities for the training and competing of healthy and successful dressage horses.

General Observations

1. Know your horse and his behaviour when he is well, especially with regard to the usual working condition of his legs and back.
2. Know the amount he eats, and his drinking habits.
3. Record his usual temperature, pulse and respiration – all should be taken when he has been resting in the stable at a quiet time of day.

Record Keeping

Keep your records of tetanus and influenza immunisation safely. Make a note in your diary two weeks prior to the required booster dates, so that you telephone your veterinary surgeon in good time for his visit. Record dates of any relevant blood tests, and future dates for worming and teeth rasping. If an appointment is necessary, make it in plenty of time and on a date a little earlier than treatment is actually due in case, for any reason, the vet is unavailable.

Feeding

There is such a variety of mixes and nuts available that it is not worth buying other types of feed unless you are buying in quantity. Those who are lucky enough to have a 'quality and quantity' agreement with a farm supplier, often receive an accurate analysis of the protein, fibre and oil levels of grain. When this is not the case, mixes and nuts which have guaranteed levels, are a better buy than poor looking oats and barley carrying little feed value.

Check the protein levels carefully, so that you don't go unnecessarily high in this area. Where hay is concerned, you are not producing a race-horse who needs to win The Derby, so continuity of quality is more important than buying the same type and from the same source.

Many horses do well enough on two feeds daily, in cases where owners are limited in the number of visits they can make each day. However, there is no doubt that the same quantity of feed will be better utilised if it is divided into three or even four feeds daily.

If the analysis of foodstuffs shows a good balance then additives other than mineral licks should only be necessary in special circumstances.

Teeth

Inspect the molar teeth, which do tend to be forgotten, regularly, rather than waiting until symptoms indicate that there is something amiss. A check-up every six months with a horse dentist or your veterinary surgeon may only take fifteen minutes of his time, and some sharp edges can be taken off the molars.

A thorough investigation is possible when a simple apparatus called a tooth gag is used. This fits onto the horse's head like his bridle, but the mouth piece is adjustable to separate the incisors and open the mouth wide. The back and roof of the mouth can then be investigated, including the molars right at the back. Sharp edges which can lacerate the horse's cheeks and tongue can be dealt with. Tiny wolf teeth, which grow in front of the upper first molars in some horses, can be quickly removed. It is almost unbelievable that these tiny teeth can upset horses in their way of going to the bridle, but they do. If you have found these teeth in evidence and there is a problem in your horse's ridden work, don't start to search elsewhere for the reason until these little offenders are removed.

When young horses are changing their incisor teeth, there is likely to be soreness in the mouth for weeks or even months. If this adversely affects your young horse's way of working to the bit, you are wise to rest him or lunge him from a cavesson without the bridle for a few weeks. Habits which become regular in connection with mouths and bitting tend to be very difficult to shake off, and remain when the cause of the trouble has long gone.

Last but not least on this subject, when your dentist has worked on the teeth, persuade him to show you how to take hold of your horse's tongue, in order to inspect the teeth more competently yourself. Then fix a diary date for his next visit.

The Back

All sorts of strains, bruises, injuries and malfunctions are simply described as a 'bad back'. Whilst the experts argue about what a horse's spine can and cannot do, it is our job, in expecting the horse to use his back well, to take good care of it. However, even with all due care taken, it is possible for a horse to pull a muscle; by bucking, slipping when getting up in his stable, or skidding to a halt in front of his field gate. With this sort of pulled muscle the horse will be lame or very uncomfortable. If it is along the top region, he is likely to show he is in pain when you are grooming.

Detecting the location of muscular troubles in other regions is definitely a specialist job, to be seen to by your vet. Remember that the earlier an injury is dealt with, the quicker it will heal. There are many forms of treatment available to speed up healing of muscles, tendons and ligaments, of which 'faradism', 'galvanism' and 'ultrasound' therapies are examples. For horses who have had muscular problems in the back, and those who have a tendency to recurrent azoturia, a piece of apparatus in panel form is available to warm up muscles before you start exercising. It is laid across the back for ten to twenty minutes before work begins.

In the case of serious injury the assistance of chiropractors and osteopaths may be required. These injuries may include any to the vertebrae of the neck, withers and back, and the possible displacement of the pelvis. When horses fall, jump awkwardly or become cast in their stables, they are often left with technically undiagnosed pain and lameness which the chiropractor and osteopath will relieve, and sometimes cure. My own view on this area of treatment is that we should not be reluctant to use it, if it is likely to succeed where all else has failed.

Cleanliness of the back and the care of the back after work require detailed attention. If your horse has worked extra hard and is very hot under the saddle, keep him walking with the saddle on, but loosened a little. Avoid removing the saddle and exposing the hot back to very cold air. In cold weather rug up the back immediately you stop working and begin walking; this means remembering to take the blanket with you when you set out to your place of work.

When your horse has cooled down sufficiently, wash down at least the saddle and girth area with warm water – again, keep the croup covered for warmth. The back is much more likely to stay free of lumps and problems caused by sweat with this procedure. Warmth is the priority after strenuous work, and for this reason many horses enjoy the treat of an infra-red lamp over their topline after hard work.

Finally, there are many numnahs available which are designed to assist in spreading the load evenly over the long back muscles. Check carefully before purchasing that they attach efficiently to your saddle, do not slip, and that they don't alter the feel of your horse's back by making you perch high above him.

Fig 43 A numnah offering total back cushioning. The filling is orthopaedic foam covered with linen which together give protection without overheating the back.

Shoeing

Farriers, quite rightly, do not take kindly to riders telling them how to shoe their horse. Your farrier will know how your horse moves from the way he wears his shoes, and most importantly will be able to detect any irregularity in the action, which he may be able to help. Remember to book your farrier every four to five weeks – another routine diary date. When your horse *looks* as if he needs reshoeing, he is overdue. When shoeing is allowed to become overdue on a regular basis, the job of maintaining the correctly balanced shape of the entire foot becomes impossible, and the farrier has every right to be annoyed if you complain.

If you explain your interest in dressage and gain his interest, your farrier may experiment with the weight and shape of the shoes to give a little extra help. The horse with weak, flat soles, and the older horse, may need cushioning on hard ground, and there are many pads and wedges available to assist. Always ask your farrier's advice: your horse will be of no use to you at all without well-tended feet.

Worming and Blood Tests

There are some highly effective anthelmintics available through your veterinary surgeon and normal suppliers. If you think, for any reason, that your horse may have a heavy worm burden, seek advice: he will probably need a blood test for worm burden, blood disorder, or possible viral infection. Which test is needed is your vet's decision.

Control of worm infestation under normal conditions is good routine management.

1. Worm every six weeks, or following veterinary advice if dealing with a problem case.
2. Remove droppings from paddocks every few days – tedious but essential.
3. If on a commercial yard, do not take on grass liveries without guarantee of regular prior-worming procedure.
4. Keep horses stabled for forty-eight hours after administration of anthelmintics. This should be another date for your diary.

Exercise

Select a goal, be it competition or a level of training, for nine months from now. Work backwards from there, slotting in intermediary achievements – outings and competitions which will be stepping-stones *en route* to that goal. Next, divide the months into training periods, balanced with roadwork, pole and jumping exercises if relevant, and rest periods.

When you commence training with a horse who has had a break from work for several weeks or more, study his condition carefully. Allow him at least two weeks of walking before you start another month's slow build-up. This may seem over cautious, but it pays dividends.

The value of roadwork and how you ride your horse out is governed by your location, the traffic flow, and the terrain. If you are lucky enough to live in the country, with hills to tackle, you have a great advantage in your effort to produce a healthy horse. If traffic safety permits, walk out on a loose rein and encourage your horse to stretch his topline. Make the walk bold and forward, especially if your horse is lazy. He will neither help his walk nor become hard in condition if

Fig 44 Hill work tackled in a good, rounded trot will open up the movement of the shoulders and encourage the hind legs to carry weight by stepping underneath the horse.

Fig 45 A weekly pipe-opener, keeping the horse on an even contact with both reins, will maintain the sparkle and enthusiasm in his work.

he dawdles. If traffic forbids this, put him on a light contact and insist that he takes the bridle evenly forward with a long, but rounded, outline. Your roadwork is detrimental to your schooling if you allow him to go incorrectly.

If you can trot for short distances on the road or ride along bridleways and grassy going in trot and canter, encourage a good way of going so that you and your horse can have an enjoyable ride, but without loss of good outline. When he is fit, and the canter can be stronger and sustained, shorten your leathers and get forward off his back. Where there is good springy going under foot, give him a 'pipe opener', in a good rhythm and on the bridle. It will put some extra sparkle into his schooling work. Work over poles and athletic jumping are other ways of ringing the changes, with benefit to your training (*see* Chapter 4).

From these different activities, it is easy to achieve a good balance of serious training and fun activities, which in no way inhibit the learning process and are likely to add to it.

4 Basic Training

Training Grounds

The place of work, where you carry out your serious schooling, will always dictate whether your training programme can be evenly spread throughout the whole year or must be restricted to certain seasons due to adverse weather conditions. However, it is possible to train your horse without a school or an all-weather surface, given certain conditions:

1. That your land is well drained – naturally or otherwise.
2. That you care for the land throughout the whole year, by harrowing, rolling and topping to promote the best possible growth of grass.
3. That you work in different areas of your field and avoid poaching popular patches.
4. That you do not overgraze the land if you want a good top to work on.
5. That you accept that the days over the winter period when you will be frozen up, and need to ride or work elsewhere, will add up to several weeks.

When you do your schooling work in a large field, break the field down into smaller areas. Mark out twenty-metre squares, and use cones or tyres to define circles of fifteen and ten metres, otherwise you will find yourself riding very large circles and shapes. This can lead to difficulties when you find yourself competing in a twenty- by forty-metre arena.

If you work on an all-weather arena or in an indoor school, make sure that you know its exact dimensions, so that you are not misled by its possibly irregular size when attempting to ride accurate circles and movements.

Working in the Arena

Work away from the outer wall or fence frequently, on inner tracks and quarter lines, so that you keep your horse straight from both legs and not simply from the inside one, with the wall for support on the outside. Plan where you intend to go, even when working in, so that looking ahead and riding well become habitual, and not something which you attempt to do only when in a competition arena. Becoming confident of the shapes which you ride, on a daily basis, is significant in helping to reduce your nerves when test riding. Train yourself to make transitions away from the outer track, for instance around a well-defined circle or on crossing the centre line.

Schooling with other riders working around you is also good training for your competition outings, where working in facilities are often overcrowded. In these circumstances you must plan ahead shrewdly, so that others see where you intend to go (because you are looking in that direction), and so that you avoid ill-prepared manoeuvres in attempting to avoid crashes with other horses.

You should show consideration for other riders in following the safety procedure when arriving at and departing from the indoor school, or any enclosed place of work. Always ask permission to enter, and wait for the go-ahead; when leaving the school, warn other parties of your intentions before you go. This will help a rider who is coping with a difficult or young horse to work out a strategy and avoid an accident.

Educating the Young Horse

The education of a young horse from birth, and particularly during the period from three to five years old, is material to fill a book in itself. Here are some of my own priorities for backing and early ridden education.

In the Stable

Your voice will be your most useful 'aid' in your very young horse's education. By taking the trouble to achieve an early respect for your vocal commands in the stable, you will have laid firm foundations for the next stage of training and will have raised a well-mannered youngster who is a pleasure to show off.

Use the following commands to ask for action: 'Stand'; 'Over', gently pushing the horse with the flat of your hand at the same time; 'Back', again gently pushing on his chest with a flat hand; 'No!', when anything is not in order; 'This one' or 'Foot' when handling his feet; 'Walk on', when leading out, and 'Whoa' for the halt.

He must also learn to stand quietly while you groom him and work in the stable, as this teaches him to be patient and prepares him for travelling.

From Three to Five Years Old

The following guidelines will help in the continuing education of your young horse.

1. Three-year-old horses should wear a bridle in the stable for ten or fifteen minutes most days of the week when you are present. Use a jointed snaffle which fits snugly. It must not drop low in the mouth; this will happen if it is too long or fitted too low.

A breaking bit, with keys on it, will irritate him and encourage an over-active mouth. This habit is likely to stay with him forever and will lose you plenty of marks in your tests.

2. He should wear a roller. If he has already worn 'pyjamas' during the winter, he should accept a roller and breastplate happily. Otherwise, find someone to help you and quietly put a roomy roller on him, with a well-fitted breastplate to prevent it slipping backwards or around him. Any new task such as this is best done after his frolic in the field, when he comes in to be fed or for the night.
3. Lead him with bridle and cavesson on, adding the roller and breastplate when they are accepted in the stable. When he is obedient to your voice, he can be introduced to a variety of situations; take care to lead him equally from near and off sides, so that he does not learn to favour being led and lunged from the near side.
4. Begin lunging work (*see* Appendix).
5. At this age, your horse should accept the weight of a lightweight rider, with the voice which he knows and respects remaining in control of the lunge and, later, of the working free situations.

When first ridden, your horse will

learn to accept light leg and rein aids if they are introduced into the system of well-understood vocal aids. Sometimes acceptance of the leg aids without vocal backing is best left until he is ready to hack with a partner, when there will be much to keep his interest and prevent him from worrying about your movements.

6. He should learn to take a lead from, and follow the example of, a well-mannered schoolmaster.

Once this stage has been reached your horse needs to cover some mileage and see the sights. He should now accept the bridle and basic aids, but there should be no fast or exciting outings yet. His objectives for the next few months are to learn to be calm, to build some muscles, and to become more experienced.

Early Schooling

A young horse runs out of stamina quickly, so he will suit a programme of schooling for ten or fifteen minutes, followed by half an hour of road walking or exercise around the farm. The schooling can take place three or four times a week, with hacking only on days in between. Increase his corn ration steadily, especially during the winter, if the frost is likely to curtail your activities. The horse who finds concentration difficult when he first comes out of his stable, will benefit from undertaking his road exercise first, to take the edge off him before his lesson. Remember that you will eventually have to school him first, so that he learns that work is required at competitions, when you demand his

Fig 46 A bold working canter ridden off the horse's back can assist in keeping a lazy pupil interested and enthusiastic in his work.

concentration.

The duration of any schooling session is dependent on several factors: the level of the horse's training, the amount of revision he needs and the new ground he is attempting to cover; his level of fitness; and his temperament.

The lazy pupil is usually better suited to work sessions which are broken down into short, sharp bouts of activity. With rests in between, his total work out may be thirty minutes, followed by some fittening exercise in the countryside. The forward seat, sharp canter once or twice a week keeps this sort of horse interested in his work.

The horse who is quick or nervous in his temperament and attitude needs more time. He frequently has the sort of nervous energy which must be slowed down into a rhythm. This, in turn, has a calming influence. The daily work session with this horse may fluctuate from forty-five minutes on an easy day, to an hour and a half when he is excitable.

Structuring the Work Session

We are working to produce an equine athlete, and like the human athlete, he should not ask his muscles to cope with serious demands until he has prepared them with stretching exercises, that is, until he has limbered up. Allocate five or ten minutes of your time to the walk when you arrive at your place of work. The psychological effect of this should never be underestimated; it allows you to loosen up your own shoulders, hips and knees as a useful start to your work programme, as well as ensuring that the walk, as a pace, is not neglected. A strong

Fig 47 A forward thinking free walk on a loose rein is the best way to stretch the topline muscles as preparation for the work which follows.

walk on a loose rein, with full use of your horse's head and neck, stretches the long back muscles and loosens his withers and neck in readiness for further activity.

The strength of the trot with which you begin is dependent on the way your horse generally 'comes out'. He may be unbalanced, because he is young or uneducated; or stiff, due to age or his way of going in the past; or ready to begin but tending to start out stiffer on one rein.

If he is stiff or unbalanced, work through big circles and easy changes of direction in a trot which is not quite your full working trot, to complete the loosening up. To ask a stiff body to work, especially at speed, is thoughtless and harmful. Your horse will be more responsive, and will not evade your aids so often if you allow him this first fifteen minutes of stretching time. Many horses benefit from some loosening working canter on each rein.

Your pattern of work from this point will be determined by temperament, timing and the level at which you are working.

Basic Foundations

The suppling period will be followed by the 'ABC' of schooling. With elementary and medium level horses this will be transitions and easy lateral work, combined with slight variations within the trot and canter, especially on large circles. All of this work is thought through, to lead the horse into his next phase of improvement which is the more difficult movements within his present level, and the learning of new work to take him up the ladder to the next.

The ABC work for the novice horse will form the essential foundations of his schooling. This work will include the improvement of his paces through transitions, variations within them, and the beginnings of sideways steps.

Whatever the timing of this – the core of the schooling session – break it into sections within itself, with at least two breathers of a few minutes of walking-off discipline. Muscles become tired and ache when they are worked hard without a break. It is therefore misguided to continue schooling a horse in an exercise he is repeatedly getting wrong. His mind may be willing, but if his muscles are not you are working against your own obstinacy! If an exercise is going wrong, it is much better to walk for a few minutes and ponder the reasons why.

A good ending is as vital as the gradual beginning. Like the human athlete the horse needs to wind down slowly and will need extra coverings for warmth in all but hot climates. This means allowing time for loosening off within your total work time, because many of you will be restricted to a tight time schedule. Five minutes of easy stretching trot, followed by a few minutes' final walking-off is necessary for all levels of horses who are working hard, but especially those whose work includes true collection, small circles and demanding lateral work.

Experiment with the order of exercises during the core session of your schooling, in order to obtain the best result from one exercise in combination with another. Move from pace to pace frequently, thereby avoiding keeping your trot and your canter entirely separate from one another. Mix and match for improved transitions and better paces.

From the daily framework, evolve a suitable weekly plan so that you inter-

Fig 48 After work it is of great value to work the horse down; he must take the contact evenly and politely and swing through his back whilst being worked rhythmically through many changes of direction.

sperse the learning days with extra-curricular activities. This, and the long-term plan, may be dogged by interruptions through illness or accident, but the unexpected must not prevent you from restyling your training master-plan and pursuing your goals. The first eighteen months of training must be sound and without short cuts. This training is the base, and if it is well done, the remainder – as far as you and your horse can go – is made surprisingly straightforward. The following guidelines are the necessary ingredients for a secure base.

The Outline

Your horse must work forward to the bridle being on the bit, in a rounded outline, shape, frame or form – the word which you use to define his body mass is unimportant. I will call it the 'outline' and stress that the importance lies in understanding the meaning of rounded outline and how to create it.

Your horse must work throughout his entire body, rather like a well-oiled machine with every part contributing. The will to go forward must be in his head, but the power emanates from active hind quarters, the hocks especially. His whole back must swing freely, carrying your weight by coming up underneath you. The impulsion created behind must travel through the horse to a positive, yet elastic contact in your hand.

The length of outline in a fully trained horse can be shortened to the extreme collection of *Piaffe*, and lengthened as in extended canter. The horse's ability to do this is developed over several years of suppling and body-building.

From the understanding of outline,

Fig 49 An advanced horse in working trot.

Fig 50 A medium level horse showing working canter.

Fig 51 An elementary level horse in his working trot.

there follow some important requirements in his manner of going.

1. He must learn to be calm, but not dull.
2. He should go forward, but with control.
3. From his work, he must become supple.
4. Throughout all one-track work he must be straight.
5. He must learn to work in an even rhythm, in each pace, throughout his work.
6. He must learn through ever improving balance how to carry himself and his rider through each stage of training.

Keep the key words *calm, forward, control, supple, straight, rhythm* and *balance* uppermost in your mind.

Basic Aids

From two seat-bones, two legs and two rein aids, a most amazing choice of aids is available. It is no wonder that horses become confused! Once you have a basic understanding of the aids available you must experiment, and through improving 'feel' you will teach yourself to apply effective, yet unobtrusive aids.

An aid is a signal. Every signal which you give must be answered. From the moment when you prepare yourself to move forward from the halt, that is, when you take up the reins and close both legs by the girth, your horse must be in front of your leg. This is the vital requirement for every movement, and in every stage of his training. Sound training is impossible if your horse is not forward between your leg and your rein.

Fig 52 This six-year-old horse is hollow through his back; he is also above the bit and set against it.

Fig 53 A six-year-old with a beautifully set on head and neck escapes easily from the bridle by going too 'deep' and behind the bit.

Fig 54 Riding the horse straight, within the corridor of legs and reins.

Whip and Spurs

The use of the dressage whip is lightly and quickly to reinforce the signal which either or both legs have applied. To this end it must be used immediately behind your boot on the rib-cage.

On the rare occasions when strong punishment is deemed necessary, you must always use a short whip which does not have a cutting action. With most horses this is effective and instigates a healthy respect for the degree of aid which you insist that he should go from. If the whip produces adverse reactions of either panic or backward thinking, then continue to carry it but correct equally quickly in another way. The choices open to you are:

1. The voice. This, however, is a limited correction, since you cannot use it in a test.
2. A follow-up, sharper tapping leg aid.
3. Spurs, which you will use to sharpen up the reaction to the aid from the leg. The danger here is over-use on some horses at novice level, creating a reliance on the spur rather than a respect for the leg.

Leg

Having established the prerequisite that your horse must move respectfully forward from your leg, there are many variations and combinations of aids which can be used in conjunction with the reins.

A positive, closing aid, with both legs at the girth, can tell the horse to go forward, straighter or to lengthen. A tapping aid with one or both legs tells him to listen or move quickly.

On a circle the legs work for the bend, in asking for the rib-cage to be giving, the quarters to follow the forehand accurately and the shoulders to stretch forwards and avoid sideways escape. The horse's way of going on the circle will dictate the degree of aid required from each leg and the timing of its use. This you will discover naturally in the process of riding for accurate lines.

The legs can be applied with a holding system of aids to ask the horse to half halt or, when maintained in this way, for collection.

In lateral work, the legs work together and individually with specific emphasis. One leg may be saying 'forward', 'bend'

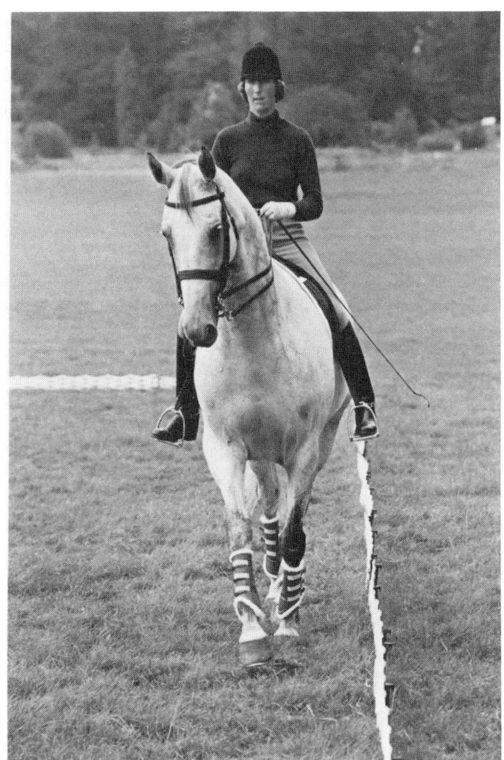

Fig 55 The bend to the right, with the horse evenly on both the inside (right) rein and the outside (left) rein.

or 'move away', or may be making all three requests at once. The other leg, simultaneously, may be guarding the quarters, keeping them active, or it may move into stronger, momentary action to terminate a movement.

These varying effects are united and controlled through good timing and clever use of rein aids. This must give the rider the sensation of his horse working 'upright', and in a corridor of control between legs and reins. In this way, hind legs and shoulders are not allowed to find escape routes, and the impulsion is channelled forward through the whole body.

Reins

There is no method of measuring or defining how much weight of contact your horse should produce in your hand. What is important, is the way in which your horse works into your reins, and the precision with which you relay your messages along them. Examine the way in which your horse, unmodified by you, arrives in your hand. This will provide you with a mirror of his present ability to work through his body. The degree to which you regulate or correct with the reins is therefore suggested to you by his way of going. Examples are the best illustrations:

1. A horse who favours working to the right because he is softer through that side of his body frequently offers too much right bend in his neck. In so doing, he sits behind that right rein contact. The left side of this horse's body is stiff and prefers that longer outside curve of the bend. Consequently he puts himself heavily into the rider's left rein, whilst not stretching through to the right one.
2. The horse who is unbalanced because his rhythm is hurried, due to hind legs propelling rather than carrying him, will throw himself onto his forehand and look for the rider's hand to support him totally.
3. When a horse is stiff and unable to use his hind legs to 'sit' into the downward transitions, he will leave those hind legs stiffly behind, and once more go against the hands, looking for support.

In each example, the horse has gone against one rein or both, due to stiffness lengthways or widthways or both, and through loss of balance. The correction must lie in following the symptom – the poor quality of contact – back to its root cause in the horse's body. From pinpointing this stiffness, the rider must work for the beginnings of equal bend through both sides of the rib-cage, and reduce the neck bend.

The rein aids with which the rider corrects must be light and repetitive on the side where the horse is stiff and heavy. On the side where he evades, the rein contact must be secure and invite him to work into it positively. In many cases where the horse sets himself onto one rein, the rider will find himself working with an outside bend in order to ensure that his horse takes up the rein which he is behind.

It is plain to see that when a horse has become very one-sided, the rider will spend some time, possibly many weeks, in riding the horse with no neck bend. He will regain better control of the shoulders and begin to create the correct bend in the body.

The rider must understand that the predominant aids for a true bend are from the inside leg forward to the outside rein. This means that the inside rein, although equally important, can be yielded lightly forward at any time as proof that it is not holding the bend. When this can be done on both reins, in all paces, then the horse is working in the corridor between leg and rein. He is then straight because he is supple, and not because he is stiff.

Half Halts

The correct use of the half halt is one of the most influential aids, through all levels of training. It has so many variants that a clear definition of the combination of signals which produce every half halt is impossible. In plain words it is a braking aid.

Imagine a small, fast Welsh pony with a small determined rider. When the rider needs to slow down, he dare not close his legs, so they remain quiet at the pony's side. The rider uses his voice and tiny, repeated rein tweaks which the pony cannot take hold of and pull against. The legs in place, voice and quick rein aids are his half halt. The very first braking aids on a newly backed and quick thinking young horse are of the same ilk. As his training progresses, that holding leg aid which I mentioned earlier (linked with collection) is very quietly introduced.

The sequence becomes:

1. Light, holding leg aids – hind legs step under.
2. Light braking aid on the outside rein – slight compression of outline.
3. Positive legs with allowing hands – forward with better activity.

Throughout the levels of training the half halts increase in power along with the rest of the horse's work, until they become effective collecting aids. At the top of the ladder, the Grand Prix horse in a highly collected canter, being prepared for a full pirouette, will receive a half halt with all aids in use. The effect of the rider's influential position will be obvious in asking for his horse's hind legs to be sufficiently underneath him to produce light and mobile shoulders for the pirouette.

The Welsh pony and the Grand Prix horse are complete contrasts, but they both illustrate effective use of the half halt in two of the many possible variants of this essential aid.

The Paces

When watching a fully-trained, impressive horse work through his basic movements with beautifully balanced yet athletic paces, it is easy to imagine that he was born with the paces which he now displays. This is not so. There are many horses competing successfully at the top levels who began their training with adequate, but not exciting paces. It is thoughtful, progressive work over several years that by educating and body-building develops the natural paces with which the horse begins.

The Walk

The horse walking free in the paddock or open country covers the ground with long, sweeping steps, in a purposeful rhythm. His movement is economical but effective. When you begin training a horse, these are the very qualities which you look for in this pace. If the horse's walk already has a calm but purposeful air about it, then you must strive to keep these assets.

The four distinct, but regular footfalls must remain regular and unhurried when you place your horse on a contact between leg and rein. When he is ridden in this way and takes the contact forward with a rounded topline, we have a medium walk. In early training you will be working him in the medium walk, the free walk on a long rein, and the free walk on a loose rein.

In the free walks you must encourage your horse to stretch his whole topline by

Fig 56 Free walk on a loose rein. For the free walk with a long rein, the same stretching must be shown with the horse remaining on the rein contact.

allowing him to reach forward and down with his head and neck. The loose rein demands this outline, with no contact, which is easy to achieve by using it as the beginning and end of all your work sessions. The long rein version demands the same outline, down and forward, with a contact. This shows the horse's desire to take the contact positively forward and down, proving that he is in front of the leg and correct in the rider's hand.

These requirements indicate clearly that the rider must allocate plenty of time to this pace, and not fall into the trap of walking only for a quick breather. The walk as a pace is the most easily spoilt, usually because insufficient care and time have been allocated to it in the horse's early training.

The most common mistake in the riding of the walk is to hurry it. The rider who is a newcomer to dressage and competition easily becomes obsessed with the fact that his horse's walk is inactive. At this stage, a great deal of over-riding from legs, body movement and anything else the rider can engineer, starts to send the horse hurrying out of his walk rhythm, at great speed. The moment that this happens, the horse has to shorten his steps in order to cope with the extra speed. Through hurrying him the rider initiates tension through the back, which is the forerunner of many of the difficulties encountered later when collection and extension are demanded from the pace.

The horse whose temperament causes him to want to rush everywhere, walking or otherwise, requires a very patient and clever rider to slow the walk to a regular, but unconstrained, level. This type of horse often produces a walk which shows steps of unequal length behind, due to his tension, and a tendency to bottle himself up and come behind the bit. He must be encouraged to walk slowly with a long neck (not necessarily down), so that the steps regain length and the rider can begin to ride the horse properly forward again from the legs, into a contact. The rider is powerless when the horse sits behind the bit.

If the comments related to your walk on your dressage sheet say 'inactive at times' you can easily correct; if they remark 'hurried and tense' you have the beginnings of a long-term problem. Never hurry the walk.

The Working Trot

A great proportion of the movements which you will teach your horse in his future training rely on a supple and rhythmical working trot. I have mentioned the way in which your horse should work from the leg to the rein, and this is essential in producing correctly used, swinging back muscles in his trot. These muscles must be worked, stretched and trained to come up under the saddle in readiness for the demands of collected, extended and lateral work which will be asked for in the training ahead.

The speed of the rhythm in your working pace must be decided by you. Some horses do give the impression that they have a built-in metronome (invariably they have a clever rider too) but most horses do not. You must ride him forward into a rhythm where he is working through a variety of shapes, with a degree of impulsion which does not cause loss of balance. If he begins to lose balance, through his corners, in his transitions and particularly by looking

Fig 57 The working trot.

for too much support from the reins, then your rhythm is likely to be too fast. Use the correct rhythm. The half halt will enable you to create good balance within the pace, by regulation but without losing impulsion. A well-developed working trot can easily be shortened or lengthened, because the base is secure.

The Working Canter

Rather like the walk, the canter can give the rider difficulties if certain priorities are not observed in the early training. The mechanics of the pace, and the horse's inclination to carry his quarters crooked (to the inside) can be particularly problematic. When we put a rider's weight on top, we must ensure that the horse is ridden straight for the comfort, balance and safety of both parties. To be straight he has to work hard, by actively bending his hocks, especially that of the inside hind leg. If this hock sneaks to the side, it cleverly avoids this hard work, and detracts from the impulsion and quality of the canter pace.

The canter is made of three steps per stride followed by a moment of suspension. The three steps, or footfalls, are:

1. Outside hind leg.
2. Outside diagonal pair.
3. Leading inside foreleg.

It is important for you to remember that although the inside foreleg appears to lead the canter, it is the final beat of the three. In all your canter training, keeping the regularity of that three-time beat is vital. This will be a particular priority when collection of this pace comes into the work, especially if your horse lacks activity and is happy to slow the canter too much. The main problem is that the three-time beat becomes four-time, by the separating of the diagonal pair. Although collection is not our concern at this moment, it is important to understand why the safety of the three-time beat is essential. Straightness and activity within a balanced pace are top of the list. Your riding, in order to achieve this, is full of important reminders:

1. The inside leg to outside rein aid influences that necessary activity of the inside hind leg, in making the hock bend and come under the body properly.
2. The half halts down the outside rein control speed and develop balance in conjunction with that important inside leg.
3. The rider's outside leg assists with impulsion. It must also guard the quarters through circles, particularly when they decrease in size.
4. The inside rein must maintain an elastic and following contact. It must never become restrictive or backwards in effect, for it will then cause a blocking effect on that inside hind leg.

One of the most common problems, both with young horses and stiff older ones, can be difficulty with striking off onto the correct canter 'lead'. The trouble is always stiffness related, but frequently develops into a question of habit.

Let us think through a well-prepared and executed transition to canter. The

Fig 58 The strike off to left canter.

Fig 59 Anne Grethe Jenson with Marzog straight in the corridor of legs and reins.

rider may choose a curved line on which to prepare and ask, so that there is already a well-established bend. The rider's outside leg brushes back a little, to ask the horse's outside hind leg to begin the canter stride. Simultaneously, the inside leg at the girth must tell him to go forward and remain straight. The reins must maintain the horse's positioning of head and neck and also exert influence on the control of the shoulders, so that they work forward in the transition and are not allowed to fall in or outward.

As when riding the pace itself, the outside rein during this transition must control the degree of neck bend. When there is a stiffness and co-ordination problem in the move off into the canter from trot, the horse usually falls onto the outside lead because he was already drifting sideways before the aid was given. If the rider has made the mistake of riding deep into a corner, this encourages the escaping shoulder still further. This is an occasion where excessive bend in the neck to the inside gives the outside shoulder even more chance to move in the wrong direction. These are some of the many contributory factors which all detract from straightness and forward movement before, and throughout, the transitional stride.

To change this habit in the preparation and strike off, it is generally necessary to keep the neck very straight between the reins. To this end you will appear to be creating an outside positioning or bend. If this causes the horse to fall onto the correct canter lead, then you are at least breaking the bad habit, which is a means to an end, and the beginnings of convincing the horse that he is capable of co-ordinating his movements into the correct lead. When the horse is incredibly stiff and these tactics have been unsuccessful, placing a pole on the ground with thoughtful use of wall, fence or hedge will produce the required result (*see Fig. 60*). The timing of the aid in relation to the position of your props is the key factor.

Lastly, you may have more success by attempting the difficult rein first. Many horses, having already cantered on their favourite lead, keep the co-ordination for that canter firmly in their minds, and so add to their physical problems.

Within the canter pace, and when asked for the downward transition to trot, horses who are very stiff in their backs sometimes evade the action of the outside rein aid by swinging their quarters to the

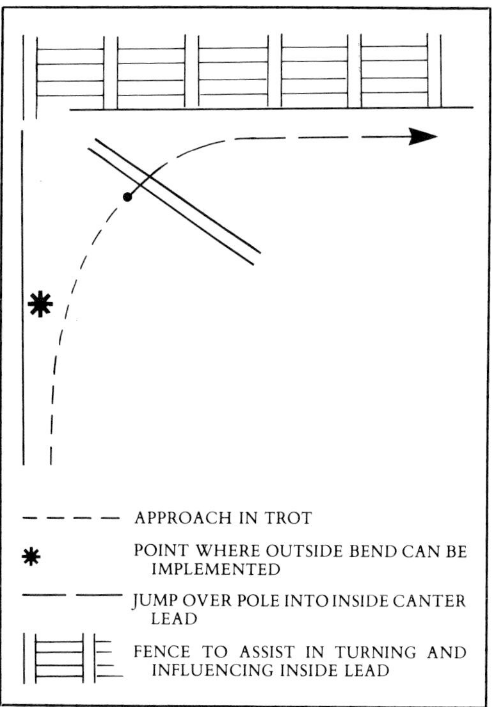

Fig 60 The use of props can help improve the transition from trot to canter.

outside, and then become disunited in their sequence of canter steps. This is very jolting and uncomfortable for both parties, and the horse may find a way out of it by falling into trot or changing his lead in front to match the offending hind leg, thereby putting himself onto his outside canter lead. Some horses will do this quite intentionally to put themselves on the lead which they prefer.

Prevention is the only cure. The rider must improve his horse's attitude and reaction to his outside rein with half halts and by assessing the quality of contact there, in all the work. Through corners, and the particular trouble spots where the habit most often occurs, the rider must maintain a stronger outside bend positioning for a time. As the habit is corrected, you may then begin through an improved canter, to work with the positioning which you are ultimately riding for. Keep the inside leg well forward to the girth, so that there is no question of you pushing the quarters out, due to that aid slipping back.

Transitions

Your horse cannot perform an active and well-balanced transition from one pace to another unless the pace which he moves from is well prepared and in good balance. Any problem of poor rhythm, erratic or too strong rein contact will be carried right through a bad transition and be there with you in the next pace. Preparation for the downward transitions, in a horse's early training, is frequently the area which he finds most difficult. The use of a circle, well and accurately ridden, with frequent small half halts, will bring the canter or trot to the best balance which the horse can produce at his stage of training.

The manner in which the horse is moving into the outside rein is of great importance. If he is secure, but light, in that rein, then the aid which asks for the transition comes through the rein clearly, and there is lightness and activity throughout the transition. This obviously gives the rider the best possible strides in the new pace, so that the transitions work for the rider and the movement comes together as a whole. Insist that your horse keeps a healthy outline throughout upwards and downwards transitions, using your half halts to see this request through. Every transition which you make is an important part of your horse's training. If you make a poor transition, then think through the causes and persevere for a better result.

Finally, to sum up the priorities of your early training, your aims should be to produce a happy, obedient horse who is always in front of your leg and straight in the corridor of legs and reins.

5 The Competition World

The world of dressage competition caters for all levels of riders and horses. We are lucky to have a large network of riding clubs who provide friendly, informal competitions, and also a regional and national scale of dressage meetings. These, and our riding schools who provide good venues, sometimes indoors with the opportunity to compete in the winter season, are a marvellous training ground for young horses. They also offer an informal introduction to competition riding to those owners who would like to give their horses competition opportunities, but think that they are not competitor material themselves. These riders often blossom into ardent competitors and frequently move on to the affiliated ladder.

Preparing for Competition

If you are keen to take your horse to a dressage meeting, be it a riding club friendly or a British Horse Society affiliated gathering, do not be afraid to enter because there are a few flaws in your work. Everyone who wants to train their horse, and compete with him in order to receive marks and comments, must make a start somewhere. When you are putting together several minutes of transitions, active trot and canter circles, plus serpentines and some straight centre lines, you are ready to compete. If you lack confidence, ask a friend or your instructor to take a video of you, so that you can appreciate the good points and see where you must work to improve.

Make a point of visiting some low-key competitions as a spectator. This advice holds true for those who are moving up a rung on the ladder, such as from elementary level to medium, in addition to those who are newly entering the competition scene. Observe how the competent riders work their horses through the movements; notice the points where several competitors make mistakes; have a copy of the test with you so that you are aware of what they should be showing at which marker. You will be surprised at the inaccuracies at all levels. Most of all remind yourself that you are a spectator, and that nerves do prevent both riders and horses from producing their best work in competition. If you are determined to compete seriously, this is an area which deserves consideration and a long-term campaign against any nervousness you are prone to. You can learn useful lessons from a rider you have seen warming up for a test impressively, who disappoints you with his arena performance. As a competitor, you must remember that the judge is marking you only when you are within the confines of those white boards; you gain no marks for good working-in.

Making Entries

You must choose your venue and your tests thoughtfully. This applies whether it is your first ever competition, your first

Fig 61 The passage.

Fig 62 The extended trot.

outing at a higher level, or simply your first outing of the season.

If you are a newcomer to competition, select a venue which is easily reached and, if possible, where you have either ridden before or observed classes, so that you are familiar with where to go and what to do. A familiar venue is much less frightening because you know before you arrive where the working-in facilities are. If you are aware of the route from there to the arena, there are no extraneous stress factors.

If you are competing for the first time at a new and higher level, particularly if it is medium and above, you should find out about facilities in advance. It is very disheartening to arrive at a competition to find either rock-hard ground with little grass upon it or a mud bath. Your horse will inevitably give you a rough ride and although a potential top-class horse should learn how to operate on inferior going, he should not be subjected to it at a new level, or on his first time out; he is likely to remember it.

The competition newcomer must choose tests which are easily remembered, and with which he is familiar. If both your horse and you are fit enough, it is wise to enter two tests at the fixture, so that you can have a less nerve-racking attempt at a second test. Competitors at medium level and above may not always find two tests suitable for them on the same day. If they do, then the horse must be fit for the challenge and the two programmes of working-in must be well planned.

If you are starting the competition season with only a few classes available to you before moving up a grade you will have to think forward to the tests at the higher level at which you hope to perform when you are preparing your entries. If you have a young or difficult horse whom you suspect needs some lunging, or extra time before his first competition, you should choose a venue where you know that there is plenty of working-in space. Lunging a horse in a limited collection ring area is not considerate to fellow competitors and can be dangerous.

Administration

At certain shows influenza immunisation certificates are required with entries and on arrival at the show. If this applies, check your certificate dates very carefully before you send your entry. Put details of tests entered in your diary, plus the date on which to telephone for your test times. If your horse will require new shoes with holes to accommodate studs, remember to inform your farrier and arrange your shoeing dates sensibly with competition outings in mind. You will not ride positively if your horse is tripping because he is overdue for shoeing.

Packing

Once you are an experienced competitor and have developed a routine for the day or two prior to an outing, you will find yourself automatically preparing and packing your equipment in a certain order. However, the first couple of competitions you attend, or a violent change in the weather, may catch you out. Here are some items which are easily left behind:

For your horse

Fly repellent (keep a tin, plus a container for mixing it in the box or trailer)

Studs and other shoeing equipment
Washing-down equipment, including sweat scraper
Spare rope
Spare tail bandage
Hoof oil or dressing and brush
Quick-un-pic (unplaiting)
Spare plaiting thread and needle in case of rubbed out plaits on arrival
Girth. You should put everything together with the saddle, numnah, stirrups and leathers with girth attached, preferably in a cover or holdall
Towels and stable rubbers
For greys you will need chalk, dettol and peroxide solution, or whatever your instant whitening kit comprises
Waterproofs
Non-slip spare reins

For yourself
Spare hair net
Black tape, or shoe lace, for your number
Gloves
Stock pin and safety pins
Spurs
Dressage test folder
Show schedule of classes

Transport Check the safety of your transport a few weeks before the first outing. When dealing with a horse who has not travelled recently, put an afternoon or two aside to practise boxing up quietly. If an easy loading horse gives a lead, and a tempting feed is offered as reward when boxed, you may be saved an hour of inconvenience and nerves on the morning of your first competition of the season. A young horse should have already been introduced to travelling short distances for non competitive 'friendlies' so that he will not have to attempt too many things for the first time on one day.

Work Before the Competition

In your work at home during the week prior to the competition, keep to your normal weekly plan. Do not replace your horse's hacking or leisure days with extra schooling as it is easy to overdo things and make him sour through over-schooling. Avoid sudden changes of equipment, for example, of bit, numnah, boots or bandages in the preceding days and particularly on the day of your tests. When work is not going according to plan, it often seems like a good idea to change a noseband or bit at the last minute, but it seldom produces a good result on the day because the reason for a last minute hitch is generally to do with the rider.

At the Competition

On Arrival

Arrive at the competition venue in plenty of time. Collect your number and check your test time, then go to the arena where you will be competing to have a fairly close look at the going. If it is a big class running over several hours you may be lucky enough to see one or two competitors riding the test. Have a copy of the test in your pocket, so that if you need to query what they are doing, you can look it up.

It is sensible to allow time to see to your horse quietly and to plan your order of preparation, including having your own clothes and equipment easily to hand. It is a good idea to have a helper to do just that and to give support. If that is not possible you have to be well organised. In this case, have your horse totally ready except for his bridle, and then put the items which you will require immediately on return from your test near to hand in a bucket: grooming or washing down tools, a sheet or rug and possibly a hay net. Then put the finishing touches to your own apparel, so that you avoid spoiling your finery by having more tasks to do.

Finally, check equipment, put on the bridle and fly repellent, on both of you if necessary. Carefully move down the ramp. If your horse is well behaved in hand, and you feel there is a benefit in leading him around the box park area for a few minutes before you mount up, then do so.

Working-in

Once mounted, double check your own and your horse's dress, then go for a good walk. Don't forget to breathe well. If you find yourself, for any reason, sitting on an excited horse who has suddenly come to life due to his surroundings, then work-in at a busy trot for a few minutes, and then walk and continue with your plan of action.

If your horse is excitable and you are not at all certain how much working-in he will need, break the work down into small active sessions, but take plenty of walks in between. Also remember that if he is not very fit, he may be full of impulsion for twenty minutes and then deflate and leave you with nothing. If you are riding two tests, then consider the first test as part of your working-in. In this way there will be some work left in him for some more useful working-in prior to the later test and for the test itself.

In the case of a seasoned equine competitor, the working-in plan must be a shadow of his everyday work out. The loosening up is vital, especially if you have travelled a long way to your show. The build-up through his lateral work must not be shortened, and neither should work on good use of alteration of the stride. Aim to produce the best extended work possible before you go into the arena. A medium or extended trot is frequently required after the move away from the centre line at C, and you may easily find yourself with insufficient resources to produce it.

If there is a movement at this level which your horse is learning quite well, but at which he has not yet reached the competition requirement, do not endanger the potential or long-term quality of the movement by forcing your horse to attempt it during a test. Try to gain as many marks as possible by producing accuracy and good differences within the paces. Ensure that each movement has a slick beginning and ending, especially the lateral work; no falling into the shoulder-in, or not quite finishing the half passes. Your whole performance must sparkle and yet not lose technical merit. When working-in, make good use of small circles and be strict with yourself about their shape and size – working-in in an open field encourages the circles to grow, after which the arena feels restrictive.

Remember to remove bandages or brushing boots in plenty of time before your test so that you do not have to stop to do this immediately before entering the arena. This can easily cause you to lose concentration. Always keep moving, even if simply walking, during those last five minutes before your test. Finally, remember to check the rules pertaining to carrying a whip.

In the Arena

As you walk or trot across to the arena, develop the habit of double-checking that the arena markers are in the correct place, especially if you are an early competitor in a class. Say 'Good-day' to your judge and give your name and number if asked. If there are any distractions which your horse is objecting to, ignore them and keep him busy with transitions, some strong trot work, or whatever work holds his attention best, until the signal is given for you to begin.

Choose a good straight approach to the arena, surroundings permitting; with a young horse keep a controlled easy trot down your centre line. Do not overdo the impulsion or you may find that you cannot halt at X. A competent horse must be ridden boldly into the arena and be kept well balanced but positively forward to his half for the salute. As you move away from X, concentrate on your breathing.

The going underfoot has a strong bearing on how much to demand from the younger horse concerning depth of corners, degree of lengthening and progressiveness of transitions down to halt. Very hard ground or mud will give the youngster a loss of confidence when he slips. Your riding must therefore be positive and inspire confidence, without being over-demanding. A horse with some experience should be sufficiently between leg and rein to be helped by the rider to maintain his stride in adverse conditions. Bear in mind that if you ride daily on a springy man-made *manège*, plain turf will not reproduce the same spring in your steps. Likewise, when going from working-in on turf into a test arena of fairly deep sand, be prepared to work hard and don't overdo your working-in in this situation.

If you make a mistake, or a movement is not well executed, do not allow this to disappoint you to the extent that you ride half-heartedly for the remainder of the test. You have lost marks for one small part of the test, so be determined to collect extra marks from there on, to make good the loss.

Always finish your test positively. Keep the young horse between both legs firmly on the final centre line. With a higher level horse, keep him collected right into the final square halt. Leave the arena in a powerful, long striding walk, on a loose rein. Keep your posture good through this final walk as you are still on show even though not being marked as such.

After the Test

There are always post-mortems after all levels of tests, and it is of great value if helpers and fellow competitors have watched and can offer advice. A video of your test, yet again, is of tremendous help for you to see how it looked and link it to the comments on the judge's sheet later. As you lead your horse back to your box, reflect upon any areas which were weaker than you expected. Consider the work which may be needed to improve the performance for the next outing, or, indeed, any exercises which can be done that day to assist, if you are riding another test. Make your horse comfortable if he is performing again. Clean him up without fuss, and let him relax with a feed, or graze him in hand, if there is good grass and sunshine. Remember to praise your horse throughout the day when you are pleased with his efforts.

In the summer months when you are arriving home at the end of a competing day in daylight, many horses appreciate an hour or two to roll and relax in their field. With a sensitive and talented performer this can be very therapeutic and worth every bit of the effort. When the weather is not so accommodating, pay attention to your horse's warmth with rugs and a good deep bed at the end of a long, tiring day. Don't forget that whilst you are driving your vehicle to and from the show, your horse is working hard to keep good balance on his feet behind you.

Hard-working, top equine competitors will benefit from a walk out under saddle the morning after a busy day. In any event, a day or two's break from schooling is refreshing before his return to work.

Planning the Season

How much any horse can and should compete in one season is debatable. A horse who is seven or eight years old and working well at advanced medium level is capable of competing through a busy summer fixture list, with a break for two or three weeks when the ground may be very hard. He is likely to compete once every seven to ten days, if the plan is to give him a full season.

A young horse may go out about once every two weeks for the first half of the season, and then have a break for a few weeks. If the ground has become very hard, it is short-sighted to ask a promising five-year-old to extend his trot, as this will cause him to lose his confidence and jar his legs. If he has been successful, he will need the break to keep him scoring points which are in line with his ability. Otherwise he will find himself graded at a higher level than he is capable of competing at. Aim to work at home at a higher level than the competition requirements, in order to be confident and proficient in the test.

Finally, always prepare well, choose your tests and venues thoughtfully, and build up steadily through the outings, keeping the homework and competitive goals evenly balanced.

Equipment

There is sufficient material in this subject to fill a book. My reason for including this section is to give some ideas and practical advice, as the equipment which you use in the stable and when working your horse, and the way in which you use it, can have considerable influence on your performance in the arena.

Bridle and Bit

Ideally your horse's bridle should match the type of head which it rests upon in its width and substance. A strong head which has character and possibly large ears does not suit a dainty, narrow bridle which would fit a show pony. If you are lucky enough to be choosing a competition bridle, take the trouble to find the width of leather which enhances a bold head, or a neat tiny head, whichever is the case.

The type of noseband which you work in will obviously have been selected through trial and error. Once again, the fit and height of adjustment on the face can help the horse's appearance or create an unflattering picture. A cavesson or flash-type noseband, which should cut a clean line across the horse's face just below his projecting cheek bone, loses its tailor-made effect if it is dropped low on the nose. A dropped noseband is difficult to fit really well to both nose and bit, unless it is adjustable across the front. Off the peg, dropped nosebands are frequently too long across the front of the face, and it is wise to measure the vital statistics of your horse's head before going out to buy.

When deciding which type of bit would best suit your horse and his way of working, the first step is to look thoroughly at the external proportions of his mouth and lips, then investigate inside the mouth. Although a large, thick German-type snaffle is considered kind, it is totally unsuitable in a small mouth. A horse with a narrow jaw, a large fleshy tongue and quite small features externally, needs a small, but not thin, pony-sized bit. Many thoroughbreds and small horses have this type of mouth and there is just not room in it for a hunk of metal.

Fig 63 A strong head which was not designed to wear a dainty bridle of narrow leather! The width and height of the noseband help to break the line of a rather long face. The size of the jaw and muzzle can easily accommodate the set of German bits which are both thick and hollow.

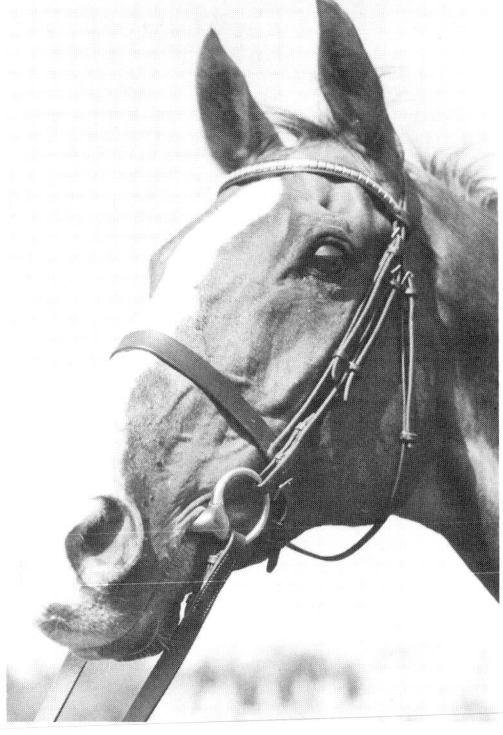

Fig 64 Pennant wears a German eggbutt bridoon, as fits his small thoroughbred mouth perfectly as a snaffle. His cavesson noseband is plain on his attractive head and fits close to give a neat, uncluttered appearance.

This sort of mouth usually appreciates a 'German eggbutt bridoon', which is technically part of a double bridle, but can be thick enough and yet still accommodate the fat tongue. A loose ring snaffle is effective but kind on horses who would take hold a little too much in an eggbutt 'cheek' variety of snaffle.

A very young horse can wear a loose ring bit from day one, provided that it is short enough across the mouth; it must not droop right forward to the back of the lower incisor teeth, and should crinkle the corners of the mouth slightly.

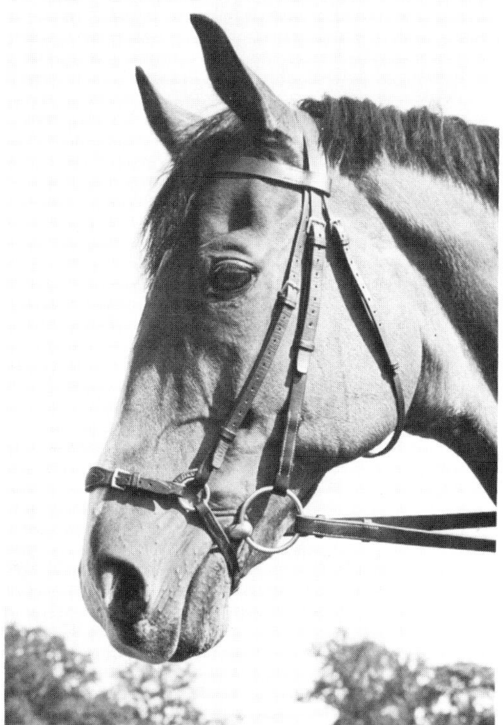

Fig 65 Caruso's dropped noseband is adjustable across the nose-piece. This enables the chin-piece to fasten without becoming caught up on the bit rings, and allows the front of the noseband to rest on the face clear of the nasal passages.

Cheek snaffles require a piece of leather – a 'retainer' to hold the upper cheek upright. They are a kind bit and will encourage a very light mouth to take a confident contact because the bit is secure and held steady in the mouth, mainly by the upper cheek and its retainer. It is, however, not good for a horse who leans against the hand, for the same reasons.

A rubber snaffle (straight mouth) can be very useful with a young horse who is genuinely soft and sensitive in the mouth. As an everyday bit for training, a straight mouthpiece of any material gives a limited feel, sometimes 'wooden' after a time of wearing it. Nevertheless, it often produces an excellent short-term effect, to change a habit or calm a problem tongue.

I have already mentioned in detail the importance of mouth and dental care, but it deserves note here once more, that if your horse is very unhappy and irritable with his bit, seek advice quickly because his reaction to the bit is a symptom of a problem in most cases.

Double bridle When the time to introduce the double bridle comes along, your horse will have completed about eighteen months of good basic training. The same set of rules which you have followed for finding the type of snaffle which suits the mouth, applies in this case. Sometimes it is necessary to mix and match to gain the result and fit needed for your horse, whose way of going to his bit you will know well by now. For instance, you may require a bridoon which is of the thick German type, but feel that to put its thick partner with it is too much of a mouthful, so it may be sensible to partner it with a weymouth of ordinary thickness.

Whatever you decide, you will need to look in the mouth and use the reins, and check from the ground how the bits lie in the mouth – bridoon snugly above the curb bit, and no trapped corners of mouth.

Browband Many horses, particularly those of a dark colour, suit metallic or coloured browbands, although this is a matter of personal choice. Similarly, matching stitching on browband and noseband can be attractive. It is a shame to spoil a well-fitted bridle by fitting rubber or cross-country reins under normal weather conditions, but on a young horse when it rains hard, safety considerations in the form of rein stops and webbing reins, are sensible.

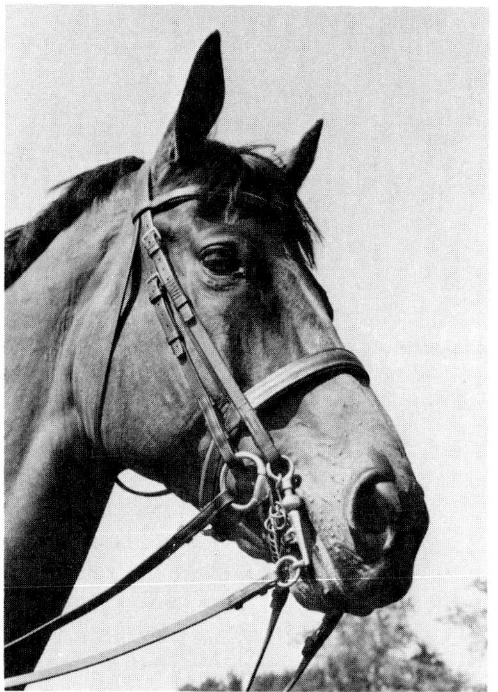

Fig 66 Falcon's double bridle has a thick German bridoon partnered with a smaller curb bit. His narrow jaw and large tongue do not allow sufficient room for the thicker, hollow-mouthed curb partner to the bridoon. The lower curb cheek is short and still remains mild in action when the mouthpiece moves up a little, as the sliding cheek allows.

Saddle

Your saddle is without doubt the most important item of all to you and your horse. The following are priority considerations:

1. That the saddle fits your horse's back in width of tree, over the withers and shoulders and in length along the back.
2. That you sit in it centrally and evenly, not to one side, as happens if a spring tree has become twisted. It must not tip you forward or backwards, even slightly, when the horse is moving.
3. That it fits you in length, with about a hand's width to spare behind your seat.
4. That the saddle allows you to feel deep in the centre of it, but must not, by its shape of flap, take any part of your leg away from the horse's sides.

Girth Tabs Long girth tabs are much more comfortable under the leg, and a short dressage girth with well-placed keepers will keep the long tabs tucked away tidily. If you are short in length of leg and tend to lift the flaps, a loop stitched unobtrusively to the inside of the saddle flap will keep it down and very close to the horse, by accommodating the girth tabs through it on their route to their own buckles below.

Numnahs There are many types of numnahs and underlays for saddles.

Many numnahs are made in machine-washable, natural fibres which are long lasting and sensible materials to have close to a sweaty back. The purpose of the numnah is to absorb sweat, but if a cushion is also required there are many good products available. For competition purposes, they should be white, and follow the line of your saddle neatly.

Breastplate A breastplate of hunting type is a good item to use in the early days of training and competing with a young horse. It is allowed, under dressage rules, and the only point against it is that it can break the outline picture at the point where it sits at the base of the neck. However, safety should be your prime consideration, so wear it with the youngster if the saddle moves or if you need the support in moments of sudden activity.

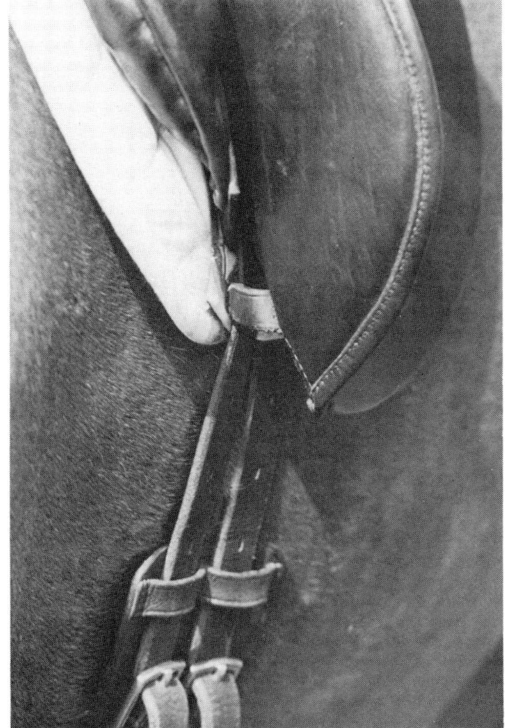

Fig 67 The saddle flap is folded back to illustrate that the long girth tabs are slotted through a loop on the inside of the flap. This holds the outer saddle flap close to the horse's side and is especially useful if the rider's lower leg or boot tends to roll the flap up.

Boots and Bandages

In the first year or so of a young horse's education, whether he is destined to specialise in dressage or not, it is practical for him to wear some sort of boots or light protective bandages when working. It is a safeguard against injury, particularly to the inner lower aspect of the fetlock joints. Many young horses move close behind when lacking muscle and still growing. They are also quite likely to buck and kick and inadvertently strike into themselves for no good reason.

Trainers who do not use boots usually claim lack of time to put them on and take them off. Nowadays there are many types of inexpensive and adequate boots available which have clips or Velcro fastenings that take precious little time to put on and stay in place well. It must be worth taking the trouble, if they prevent an injury which could keep a horse off work for days or weeks.

When a horse begins to work more seriously, and lateral work, collection and extended work are regular parts of his repertoire, protection of his legs is advisable. It is not necessary or desirable to choose boots which are supportive of the tendons, because your dressage horse cannot use that support for his competitive work. To build a support system, and then remove it in competition, is dangerous.

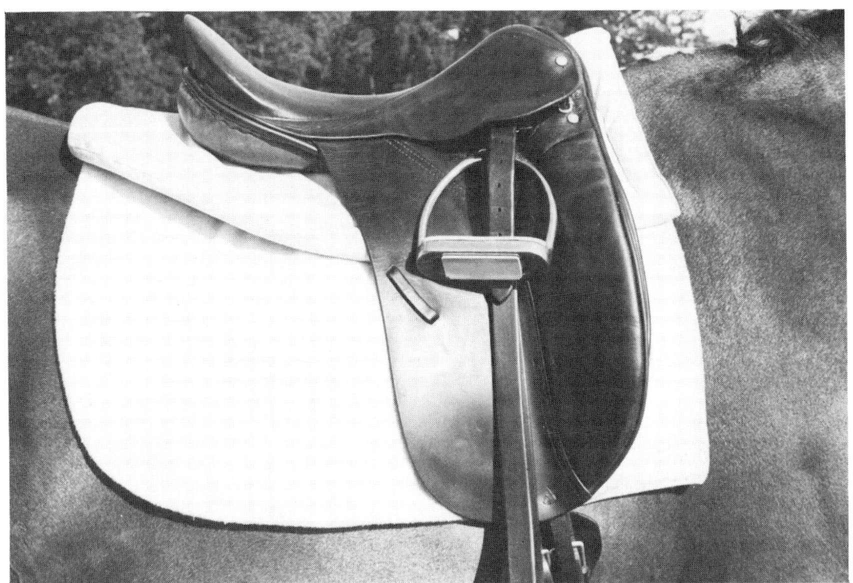

Fig 68 Working equipment: a soft cotton numnah placed under a back cushion to absorb sweat, in this case used on an older horse with a very high wither; a saddle with an overgirth which is attached to the bottom of the flap and which fastens to an extra, elasticated girth buckle keeps the saddle flap close to the horse.

Fig 69 A hunting breastplate; on this young horse it is used as a rider neck strap. When the breast ring to girth section is two to three holes tighter, it is used as normal, for securing the saddle for hill work and fast work.

There are many well-made bandages available which fasten easily and securely, and have their own built-in cushion layer at the start of the bandage to dispense with the need for gamgee underneath. When the bandage is so used for protection, it must have a percentage of stretch fibre in it because it has to be applied in a shaped and well-overlapped manner to the inner aspect of the fetlock joint and remain in place through plenty of activity.

The use of stable bandages for warmth, as a circulatory aid, is necessary for some hard-working legs. Where there is an intermittent problem of filled legs, check

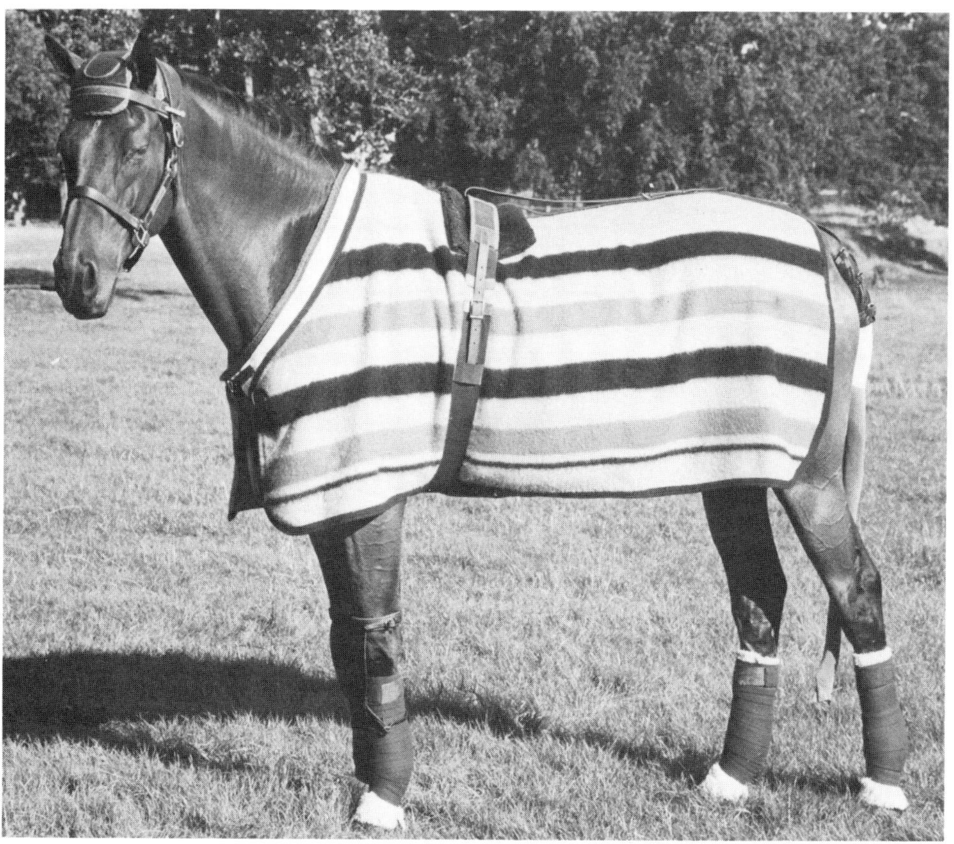

Fig 70 Ready to travel; a woollen day rug on top with a strong, cotton rug underneath to trap the warm air from the horse's body and to prevent sweating. Bandages must protect the coronary band and the tail has a guard and a stocking in addition to a bandage which should not be too tight. A horse who sits on his rump when travelling may also require hock boots. Care must be taken that the firm top straps of hock and knee boots do not rub or restrict circulation. Poll protection is advisable for tall horses, or where headroom is limited.

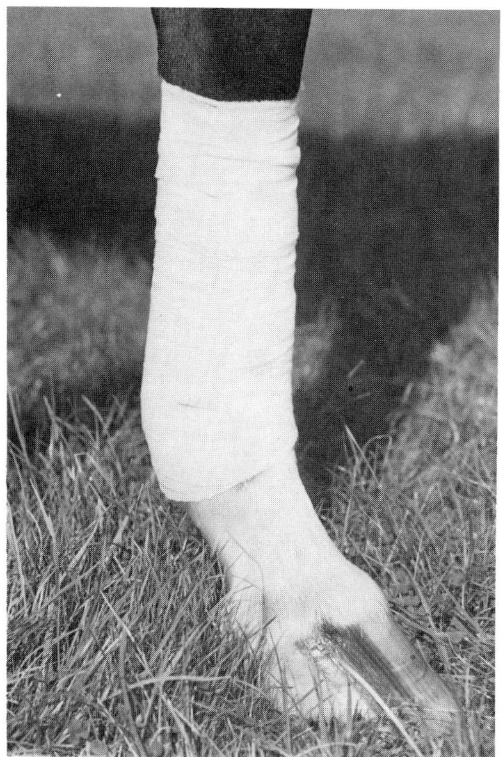

Fig 71 A well-applied working bandage which protects the inner aspect of the fetlock joint. The tapes are tucked away, high up on the outside of the bandage. They should never be tied on the inside if they are work, stable or travelling bandages.

the diet and exercise programme first, before starting to bandage. When overnight bandages are being applied on a long-term basis, the legs can become marked, so care must be taken not to bandage too firmly. Glentona thermal bandages are excellent in this respect, as they are very long and do not require an underlay, due to their thermal properties which work well when the bandages are put on with very light pressure.

Conclusions

In the competition world there is much hard work and preparation to be done in order to participate well. So much can be learned through this participation, from your own experience and from watching fellow competitors and exchanging training methods and ideas with them. Your training and competitive riding are nevertheless dependent upon care, equipment and good presentation, all of which will help you to display an impressive array of skills and achievements.

6 Strengthening the Base

After two to three months of active and accurate ground work in the working paces, your horse should be feeling more supple, straight and generally stronger, and ready for more learning.

He should be tackling twenty-metre circles in his working trot and canter paces without wobbling or escaping through either shoulder. There must be ever-improving transitions between the working paces. The free walk can be liberally alternated with the other paces. The medium walk should be gaining power and the rider's following hands must encourage plenty of movement of the head and neck, whilst the horse becomes better in his attitude and his acceptance of that contact, and takes it forward boldly.

Many horses at this stage will be capable of walking ten and twelve-metre circles or half circles in their medium walk, with active forward steps and a good bend to the inside leg. A well-balanced young horse will also cope with fifteen-metre circles in both his trot and

Fig 72 The half halt assists in transitions within the paces, for example collected trot to medium trot, and in changes from one pace to the next.

his canter, and these are all indications that he is ready to have more asked of him. The half halts must continue to assist the riding of smooth, well-balanced transitions, because he is approaching the stage of training where easy transitions within the paces will be required. These boost the quality of the paces further. Ride progressive downward transitions to the halt, and be sure to keep still but with the aids 'on him' at the halt. Choose a time in the lesson when it will be possible to keep his attention.

From this time onwards, one or two well-ridden transitions to halt should come into each schooling session. Do not overuse the side of the school for support, but use inner tracks or lines across the school where there is a marker to assist you.

Strengthening the Back

As we approach a stage of training where there will be extra demands placed on the horse's back muscles, it becomes even more important to find ways of keeping his back supple. Here are two excellent ways of doing this which can also be a recreational type of work for your horse.

Fig 73 The rider, light on the horse's back, encourages the horse to take the hand forward and down and to bring his back up with plenty of swing and a powerful stride.

Stretching the Topline

This is the equine version of the 'whole body stretch' exercise, which I hope you are working on daily! If you can ask your horse to stretch his topline in a way which can be used effectively on a regular basis in his training, it is a great asset. Few horses do not benefit from this type of work, but an example of just such a horse is one who is very loaded in his shoulders and finds it difficult not to be on his forehand. He can be worked to stretch out and forwards, but not downwards too much. His poll can come level with his withers and in this way the topline is stretched but he is not allowed to go onto his forehand.

Working Down

Working down is carried out in the working trot and canter, with a good rhythm. The horse must be encouraged by the rider's hands to stretch forward and take the rein politely down, working his topline in a very rounded and swinging way. The rider's timing of rein aids, and the way he follows the horse as he begins to respond to the aids, demands much skill which will develop as the whole exercise becomes more familiar ground. The rider may lower the hands in following the head and neck and will find an 'open' inside rein useful to encourage that same stretching. The rein is 'opened' by light direction from the rider who moves his inside hand and forearm about six inches away from the withers, towards the circle's centre point. The hand must not pull down, but simply direct clearly, and then allow the horse giving the correct answer to come through forward and down. To this end your position must be a more forward seat, and it is useful to shorten up your leathers a hole or two. This will enable you to remain light, both in rising to your trot and when off his back completely in the canter.

Pole Work

Pole work adds interest to the proceedings and makes the horse work more on his coordination and concentration. It also encourages better use of his hocks and shoulders, as his stride produces more lift.

Start with individual poles, dotted about your working area, and insist that he works over the single poles in a good rhythm. If he hurries, approach the poles on a circle line. Gradually build up a sequence of poles, beginning with two, with a three-metre gap between, and progress until he works happily over three and later five poles, with approximately one and a half metres between each. You must be prepared to alter the distance a little, by rolling the pole, to produce a longer stride if necessary. Your sets of pole exercises can be fanned around the circumference of a half circle across the school to make him bend, in addition to the stretching. If you link several changes of direction over sets of poles with bending and stretching in all directions, the work will greatly benefit his back by making it swing.

Athletic Jumping

It is good for potential Grand Prix stars to do some fun jumping and combined training during their first year or two of work. Much can be achieved by clever placing of poles into small spread fences, to teach a good athletic jump from the

Fig 74 Dutchwood (by Dutch Courage) learns to negotiate poles to improve his trot.

Fig 75 Using a three-metre placing pole prior to the jump from the trot, the horse becomes neat and quick in his technique with shoulders and forelegs and has good stretching in his neck. The young dressage horse who jumps calmly often benefits from participation in some novice jumping or combined training classes.

beginning. The horse should be jumping mainly from trot, with a pole placed at about three metres from the jump, to discourage him from standing back and cheating, rather than getting close and accomplishing some quick, neat leg work.

Build up carefully to grid work over fences; this encourages agility and a good shape in the air. Use the grid work to assist his way of going. If he does not like to lengthen, gradually pull out the distances once he knows how to cope with the fences, so that he has to stretch and meet the length. Alternatively, if he prefers to go long and avoids shortening himself, shorten the distances very carefully.

Encourage him to canter away from his fences well and straight. If he lands on the incorrect lead for a corner ahead, put your weight to the inside and ask him, with a few taps of the outside leg and a light brush of the whip, to change his lead to the inside as he approaches the point where he knows he must turn. At this moment, when he is enjoying himself and his canter is active and forward, a change will easily be given to you – with very little thought behind it, which is exactly what we want. Never discourage a young horse who enjoys attempting flying changes of his own accord, as you will be glad of this talent in a year's time.

Collection and Extension

Ultimately true extension is dependent upon the quality of the collection in each pace. It is wise to keep this point foremost in your mind, so that you aim to improve both simultaneously. You will already have a good idea of which of the two your horse finds the easier to accomplish naturally. You must not allow him to overdevelop his favoured variation of the paces and avoid the less easy option during his everyday work. Even in the novice level tests, a few lengthened strides are asked for, so at this level you must start preparations for shortening the stride, so that lengthening does come from behind and not from an exaggerated action of the foreleg, which will be of no value in your programme of sound training.

The Trot

The exercises which will produce these active, but shorter, steps and will gradually encourage your horse to bend the joints of the hind legs and carry more weight there, are smaller circles, down to ten metres. When these are accurately ridden in the trot, they begin to have a shortening effect from the size of the circle itself, so this simple exercise to produce slight shortening and lengthening is beneficial.

Work a twenty-metre circle at the A or C end of your school in a full working trot. On approaching your centre line marker A, use your half halts for preparation and ride on to a ten-metre circle. Your horse will have to be working through both sides of himself with control to begin the circle accurately. If he is kept strictly to the ten-metre size, the trot will collect a little. On completion of this circle, ride boldly in your working trot on to the twenty-metre circle once again. Then proceed to work the two circles centrally from E to B. Finally ride the exercise at the C end. If you work the exercise on each rein, you will have achieved many transitions to a shortened trot, followed by the return to a working trot, or even a lengthened stride or two. Your horse will begin to join in with the purpose of the exercise, and you will achieve the objective of some shortened steps and a few longer ones. In doing so you will enhance the quality of the working trot.

The Canter

The canter work can follow a similar pattern. The smaller of the two circles may be fifteen or twelve metres in diameter to accommodate the canter pace. If your horse is responding well to the half halts to shorten the canter, then aim for the twelve-metre circle and keep your legs on, as you use those half halts. Use the impulsion which you have accumulated to ride him forward and out onto the twenty-metre circle. Do not allow the canter to quicken or flatten. The bolder steps must be as round and coming up off the ground, as the shorter steps.

A pattern of alternately shortened and lengthened strides, in both the trot and the canter, can be ridden on a twenty-metre circle in the centre of your arena. This tests your circle riding and puts your shortening aids slightly more to the test because there is no small circle to make it happen. Keep the feeling of your horse being straight between the reins, so that you have only a little bend to ensure that you work both sides of your horse evenly. This is especially important in the trot so that you do not create too much bend to the inside, and so over-ride the length of step taken by the outside diagonal.

Early Lateral Work

Leg Yielding

The main exercises which contribute to early collected work involve some lateral work – however simple – to begin to accustom each hind leg to stepping under the body and weight carrying. Leg yielding is the simplest form of 'stepping under' exercise. It can be ridden in the walk, to show your horse the requirements from the aids slowly and quietly. In the trot the leg yielding will be ridden in a good working rhythm. Therefore,

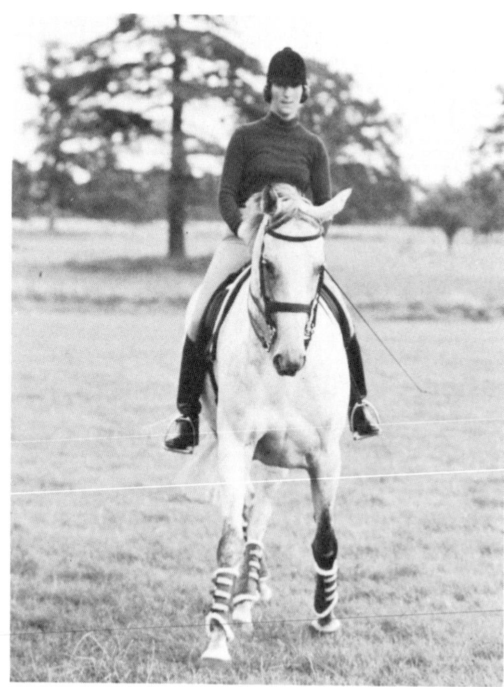

Fig 76 Leg yielding from the rider's left leg, moving forward and to the right. Notice the left hind leg stepping well under and across, whilst its partner, the right foreleg, stretches forward and to the right. Ditton is even and secure in the corridor between the reins.

although leg yielding can help in the work towards collection it is not ridden in collection. For this reason, it can slot quite easily into the novice horse's training.

Leg yielding also differs from the ensuing lateral work in that the horse is kept straight through his neck. There can be a very slight positioning of the head away from the direction to which you are riding forward and over, but this suggestion always provokes the novice rider into creating too much neck bend, followed by an escaping outside shoulder. Aim for straightness between the reins,

Fig 77 A side view of leg yielding. The rider's inside (left) leg asks for the stepping under and over from the left hind leg whilst remaining at the girth.

and you will probably ride a useful movement where the forehand is controlled and the inside hind leg steps under the controlled unit effectively.

Where should leg yielding be ridden? The safest learning route is from one straight line to another; for example, ride the quarterline and make a few steps of leg yielding towards the inner track. You are, in doing this, riding a tiny portion of a diagonal line. The control of the shoulder which is leading is vital, so at each step across you must know that you can ride forward out of the exercise. If you cannot do that, then you have lost control. The aids are to ride both sides as always, with good timing of the half halts with the outside rein. The 'asking', predominant inside leg is used by the girth. There is no need to take this leg backwards as you are not pushing the quarters over, you are asking the inside hind leg to step forward and underneath the body. If you have completed the earlier lessons of good reaction to the leg and the half halt has been mastered, there will be no problem in your horse understanding.

Your outside leg in all lateral work is as important as its partner. If the leg is back behind the girth, it is having a greater influence on the quarters. When it is by the girth, you can especially affect the stretching forward of that outside shoulder. You should make much of your horse the first time he gives you the answer you require.

When you feel competent in these aids and the result feels controlled and forward, you can attempt the same 'activating' steps in different parts of your arena. For instance, you can enlarge a segment of a fifteen-metre circle with two or three sideways steps. This is a very useful exercise, but it must be ridden

Fig 78 Bold forward riding in medium trot opens up the shoulders. This work is interchanged with spells of lateral work to keep up the impulsion.

accurately, because the arc to which you are moving out is no longer a clearly defined line, as the inner track was. You must therefore have a starting and finishing point in your mind, and look forward to your points of action in a disciplined manner.

Alternate plenty of positive, forward riding with spells of lateral work, so that the sideways steps produce the push to go forward, and the strong forward work, in turn, puts impulsion back into the lateral work. This pattern must be followed through all development of the collection and extension.

While riding your lateral work, check carefully that you are central in your saddle and upright in your body, asking observers to confirm this for you. One or two lessons on a good schoolmaster horse at this stage will be of great value to your own straightness and will assist you in understanding fully the new techniques you are using. Riding a better-trained horse will remind you of the feel which you are seeking, particularly at the start of your collecting and lengthening exercises.

The Canter

Your canter work must continue to make equal progress. If you work out in open fields, I hope that you will already have used the space well by making shallow loops of three to five metres in depth as you move around your field in working canter. When riding any size of loops in canter you must keep these guidelines in mind:

1. You must maintain the shape of the loops, that is, the strides of counter canter, by means of your usual canter aids

and not by exaggerating the neck bend. The straightening influence of the inside leg and a well-utilised outside rein is of prime importance in ensuring the success of the exercise through better use of the inside hind leg and the improved balance which that produces.

2. Your body must remain in its counter canter position, and you should not be tempted to twist your body in order to maintain the counter canter. Keep stretching downwards with your inside leg so that you do not move away from the inside riding aids, even though they are, in the counter canter, on the outside of the movement.

3. Keep the rhythm constant through the outside rein. It is essential that your horse remains upright and controlled through his forehand.

4. Within this rhythm the three time beat must stay true. Your good use of half halts and sympathetic position in the saddle must encourage your horse to stay supple and elastic through his back.

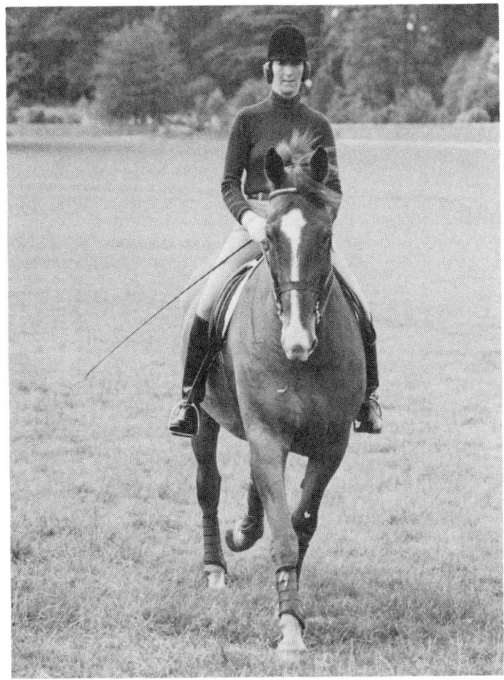

Fig 79 Working in the open field, with some help from the fence line (about two metres away to the left of this illustration). Working in the counter canter right, Dansker remains in the bend around the rider's right leg. The right hind leg is well under him and remains straight, following the direction of the right foreleg.

All these priorities serve to emphasise that counter canter is a valuable suppling exercise, but only when ridden in a way which improves the canter pace. If you struggle to make your horse maintain counter canter, through any shape or movement, by fixing him with tight reins and a strong neck bend, then you will stiffen him through his whole body and spoil your canter work as a result.

Counter canter can also be asked for using the slightly collecting influence of a twelve or ten-metre half circle to start the exercise. From this shape, which is easily produced from your quarter marker at the end of a long side, pick up a gradual incline to the long side which you have just left. Then maintain, without a struggle, a few easy strides along the track. Do not allow the canter to become hurried or falling on the forehand. Use plenty of light half halts as you return to the track, with your outside leg quietly saying 'keep this canter lead'.

The transition from counter canter to trot is very important. You must prepare it well from the counter canter, keeping your legs and reins working as if to collect your horse for two or three strides before you give the aid to trot. From this preparation, a good transition followed

Fig 80 Returning to the track in counter canter left. The rider's body is positioned slightly left, with the outside (right) leg lightly positioned behind the girth to maintain the canter left aid.

instantly by well-balanced trot work, can be achieved every time. Your horse can do all the work – the half circle in canter, a straight line of canter in balance, and a good transition down. This is really an exercise for you, the rider. You must put the pieces together expertly and your horse will give you the result for which your sound training has prepared him.

This work will put your horse much better to your straightening aids and improve the chances of keeping him truly straight in all his canter work. You must ride inner tracks and quarter lines in the canter work, sowing the seeds for well-ridden, straight centre lines, in tests to come.

Forward to the Walk

The work in the walk, especially the medium walk, must continue to receive its fair share of attention. There must be spells of the medium walk, following accurate lines, between the new ground covered in trot and canter.

This walk remains work, in contrast with the early stages of training where on most occasions the walk was on a loose rein for total freedom. The loose rein walks are still there in abundance, but he must not expect them after all strong trot or canter work. If your medium walk is bold and he takes the bridle well, you can start early preparations for the demi pirouettes in the walk.

Start by marking out with cones or tyres the four tangent points of your twenty-metre circle at the C marker. Ride the whole circle, true first of all, then imagine the circle divided into two differently shaped halves. The half across the open school remains a half circle. The two quarter arcs at the C end become straight lines, from C to their respective side tangents. Your aim will be to ride a forward going, medium walk around the rounded half circle. As you approach the side tangent on the arc which began at X, you will straighten up, staying in medium walk. As you approach the side of the school, you will ask for the walk steps to shorten just a fraction from your half halts. You must turn to align yourself with the C marker and, keeping the inside leg by the girth, increase the outside leg. With both hands moving fractionally towards the C marker direction, ask the forehand to come round to face C, on a straight line to it. Your horse will have stepped over towards C with the outside shoulder for one or two steps only. You must maintain an effective inside leg which increases to say 'enough, straighten up, forward' as you align with C.

Your inside leg is the most important aid, as training over the months ahead builds walk collection and the demi pirouette from it. This is because, in the walk pirouette, the walk must be maintained in its four clear and separate footfalls. In this early ground work, do only two or three easy attempts on each rein on that half circle-half square. Make sure that the walk on each side of the shortening and moving of the forehand is very positively medium (*see Fig 82*).

Follow this new area of learning with some active forward work in the canter, such as the twenty-metre circle with shortened and lengthened strides.

Work from the Ground

It is wise to start preparation for the rein back between good novice and elemen-

Fig 81 Don't forget the loosening off in between the more strenuous work sessions which are now part of the regular training.

tary level. This is because you must progress slowly with this exercise, as, like the walk pirouette, if it is rushed through in the early stages and spoilt technically it is in many cases irreparable. The easiest way to follow up your training for the rein back in the stable is to continue it in your *manège* or in a corner of your field.

When you have done part of your regular work pattern and reached the stage of a free walk break, ride to a square halt and dismount. Make much of your horse, but don't run up the stirrups or bring the reins over his head, as these routine actions are an indication that you have ceased work. Simply walk with him along the track or hedgerow of your field. Keep him stepping forward, with your left hand about thirty centimetres away from his jaw and your fingers lightly over the top of the reins, thumb nearest to you. Your dressage whip is in your right hand. You should plan to make a few halts and walk on, transitions, and to familiarise him with very early work 'in hand'.

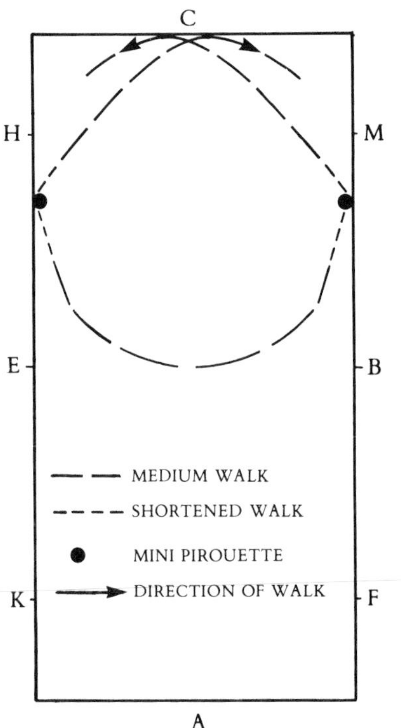

Fig 82 Laying the foundations for pirouette work in the walk.

When you would like him to halt, begin your verbal command and simultaneously move yourself forward; turn to position yourself facing him head on, with one hand on each rein – a light contact each side. He learns from this that when you are alongside him, he must move forward actively and that when you require the halt you will use the command and halt him with body positioning. The essence of the lesson at this stage is for him to understand that this is work, although you are dismounted. He will also learn that he must be obedient to those two basic commands 'walk on' and 'halt', as a forerunner to the next command which will be 'back', with your body position emphasising the direction.

Current Level

By this point, you will have a varied and interesting pattern of work. There is some stretching of the topline, lateral work, variation of the paces and some extra work for both the canter and the walk. Your horse should now be working confidently in his tests in competition, probably at the top level of novice and attempting some low-key elementary tests. To compete well at elementary level now is a matter of consolidation, and learning to work hard and well within those white boards. Your early training is finally coming together.

Fig 83 Opening up the paces by using some bold forward canter work in the open field.

Fig 84 Teaching the horse to walk in hand. The stirrups are down to indicate that he has not finished his work session. Continue with further riding after this exercise.

7 From Elementary to Medium

You will have laid the foundations for medium level work in each pace over the period of six to nine months during which you have been training seriously. Where weather and ground conditions have delayed your training, this period may have been longer. However long your basic work has taken, if it has been thorough you will make progress surprisingly quickly in the work which follows.

The objectives now are to progress from shortened strides to early collection, and from the collection to produce medium and extended strides in the paces. To do this, the lateral work, which in the future will be ridden with true collection, must be started as part of your development plan. Increased suppleness through the body will make smaller circles, better quality and more direct transitions possible, whilst providing the ground work for full extension of the paces in the future.

Shoulder-in

Shoulder-in differs from the leg yielding, which you have used as your preparation for it, in two major ways. Firstly, shoulder-in requires a bend through the horse's body. Secondly, it requires true collection. These requirements mean that the movement is a difficult one to execute with control and balance. On the other hand, it is one of the best exercises for suppling a trained horse, once the learning stage has been successfully mastered.

In the early stages, the horse is worked into the exercise in the shortened trot which we have already developed. As he becomes more proficient, the shortened steps, with improved impulsion, balance and control, become collected steps.

Technical Requirements

Shoulder-in is ridden with bend, collection, and at an angle which puts the horse on to three tracks as he moves along a straight line. Imagine the three tracks as old-fashioned tramlines. Looking at your horse from the front in his shoulder-in, the outside diagonal pair are on the middle line, with outside foreleg masking the inside hind leg and the outside hind leg on the outside line; the inside foreleg is on the inside line.

The first important fact to acknowledge when you begin to ride shoulder-in is that the angle at which you bring the forehand in from the line of the outside hind leg is very small. If you fail to appreciate this, you will make the common mistake of trying to create an impossibly deep angle for your horse to maintain, and problems will occur.

Check your levelness in the saddle before you begin. Then attempt a few steps of shoulder-in, in the walk. Ride through the short side of the school onto the inner track – of one metre in, on the long side. Have your horse walking positively into his bridle, with him even in both reins and your outside rein and leg working quietly for full control of his outside curve. Turn your upper body slightly in towards the centre of the school, and as you do so, bring your horse's shoulders a little to the inside of your track. Both reins are instrumental in achieving this, so do not over-use the inside rein. Neither hand must move backwards towards your body, as this shortens the neck and stops the impulsion coming right through the horse. Look down the line you are riding along and think forwards not sideways. Ask for a few steps only. Your aim is three or four well-executed steps with a good entry to the movement and control throughout,

Fig 85 Learning to shorten the frame.

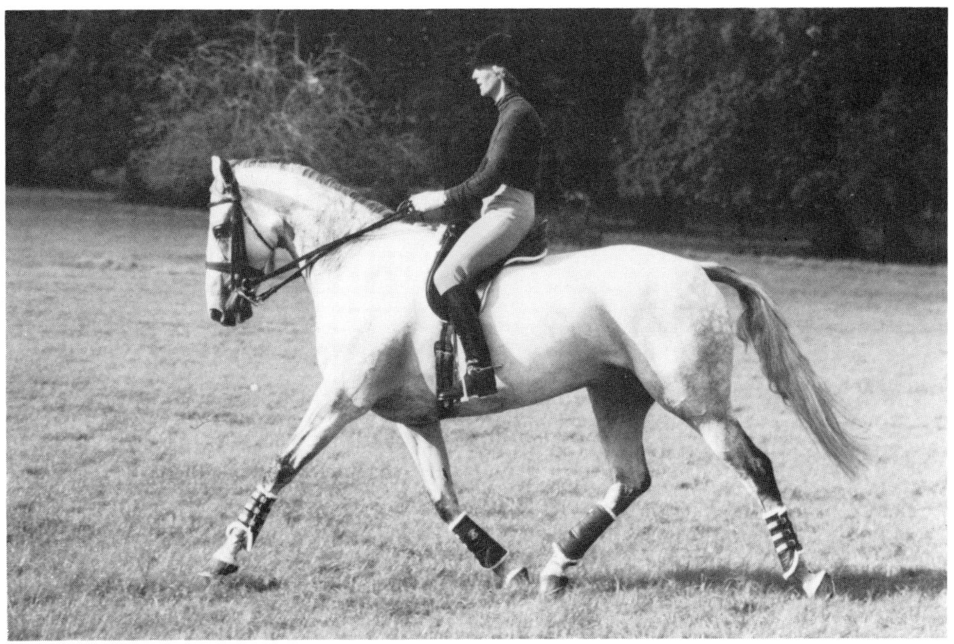

Fig 86 Learning to use collection to develop the medium and extended variations of the pace.

The build-up to shoulder-in

Fig 87 The positioning of the forehand whilst the legs remain moving along one track. This may be ridden on the inner track to test the horse and rider's ability to maintain the line without wobbling.

Fig 88 Very slight displacement of the forehand so that four tracks are seen.

including asking him forward out of the exercise after these steps.

Your line out of the movement can be a continuation of your present positioning, onto a large half circle across the school. Alternatively, after a straightening of the forehand with your outside rein, close both legs equally and ride a straight diagonal line into the centre of the school. It is important to have maintained the upright feeling through the horse's shoulders and the controlled forward movement of the outside one in particular.

Follow this simple early shoulder-in exercise on each rein, moving away from the exercise in a bold working trot so that you keep up the forward thinking. If you know that you have any serious walk problems, then obviously proceed straight to the trot build-up of the exercise. The walk beginning is simply a helping hand for the rider who is new to the work, and sometimes for the horse who misunderstands in the trot or is too quick for his rider in some way. Proceed to the attempt of a few steps of shoulder-in in the trot, along various inner track

Fig 89 The shoulder-in left on three tracks, with bend and collection.

Fig 90 Shoulder-in right, showing the right hind leg stepping well under the body, an essential part of the collecting process.

lines. In choosing a line away from the wall or fence you are forced to pay attention to the efficiency of your outside aids. It is a common problem for the horse to fall out over his outside shoulder, by losing control of his forehand, which is the essence to the whole exercise. As your horse becomes more proficient, you will find yourself using both legs equally to think more forward and less sideways. This line of thought is vital in all the lateral work which is about to occupy a large portion of your work programme. For this reason, check your own position endlessly, both in and above the saddle.

Over the period of weeks and months ahead, you must now develop the collected trot in conjunction with the shoulder-in. Improve your horse's control, going into the movement without wobbling and show improved variation of the trot work by riding boldly out of the shoulder-in with lengthened strides. When you have this feeling of control in each phase of the movement, you can safely begin to ride it on the outer track. You should also find yourself capable of choosing a line across the school such as

Fig 91 Pennant, a neat and compact thoroughbred, practising his shoulder-in.

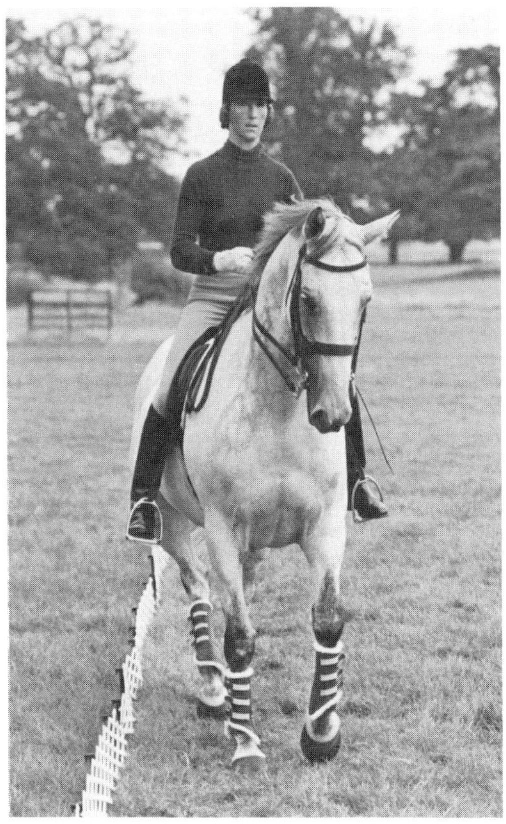

Fig 92 Ditton, with his large frame to control, benefiting from his shoulder-in work.

E–B, and riding a few steps of shoulder-in on a not so clearly defined line.

At this stage, which may take you a few weeks or months to attain, the shoulder-in should be having a very good influence on the remainder of your work. The power in the strides out of the shoulder-in should be approaching medium trot. Whilst you are tackling the learning stages of the lateral work which requires collection, do not spend continuous periods of time attempting the shoulder-in. Alternate it with other work, so that your overall work benefits and you do not become too intense with the new and difficult work.

Medium and Extended Work

The medium strides in trot and canter will be developing well from the work which you are now undertaking. However, it is essential to understand when you are showing medium paces and what the differences are between the medium and extended paces.

The Walk

In the walk, our medium example is our working pace, that is, on the bit, marching forward but not lengthening the stride. This leaves us with only an extended walk to show as our most lengthened variety of this pace. Your horse should be ready now to show some extended walk – or the nearest that you can achieve at present. It is certainly time to ask for more serious demands of the walk. The aids should simply ask for more, with good timing of your leg aids to encourage longer strides rather than faster ones. Your hands must move, not only to follow the movement of head and neck but to encourage them to be used fully. The contact is maintained throughout, and the topline should be well stretched; lower than in collection, but not downwards in the direction of working down.

It is helpful to the horse, particularly a horse who is inclined to break into trot rather than stretch, if you apply leg and rein aids in a very rhythmical manner to persuade him to be secure in his rhythm and not to break. The more supple and athletic he is in his back, overall, the less likely he is to become tense in it and then try to escape into trot.

Practise walking on an accurate ten-metre circle in the corner of your arena, having left C or A behind you. Go from this rounded active medium walk on to the diagonal line, asking your horse to stretch and lengthen his whole body into the best extended walk which you can maintain consistently. When you wish to bring him back to medium walk, keep the leg aids lightly on and use your half halts, coupled if necessary with a slight shortening of the reins and of the topline. Do not neglect the return transition, because there must always be one. This is the part of any exercise which always tests how much a movement has been in balance and on your leg; when a horse has lost balance on to the forehand, it is impossible to bring him back on his hocks for the return to the working or collected pace.

The Trot and Canter

When working the trot and the canter you must know the speed and rhythm which are your working pace. Again, the criterion of your working pace is whether you can shorten or lengthen your stride with equal ease. Bearing in mind your working stride, work both your trot and your canter around a twenty-metre circle. Ideally place the circle where you have the least wall support. On the circle, from the positive working pace, shorten with impulsion using your half halts and keeping your horse balanced and straight. Each hind foot should be following the track of its lateral forefoot.

From the shorter steps, where your horse's frame must feel compressed, ask him to work from behind with stronger, more urgent leg aids. Regulate the speed through your outside rein half halts. It is vital that you do not allow the pace to quicken with sudden and unbalanced acceleration. The strides must become increasingly longer with no increase of speed. Your hands should follow the slight stretching of topline but wait until the hind legs begin to produce it before you start to do this. Do not lose quality of contact through the change within the pace. This is a vital part of keeping the lift and impulsion within the stride and a contributory factor in bringing your horse back to the working or collected

Fig 93 The medium trot around a twenty-metre circle: powerful, lengthened strides which maintain roundness.

pace.

To produce the medium strides in the trot and canter, you are aiming for a powerful degree of lengthening which is rounder and less than the maximum which can be produced, which is your extended pace. However, the medium trot and canter is the maximum which can be produced on a twenty-metre circle with balanced, even strides.

The extended variation is shown on the long sides and diagonal lines of your arena. You have the knowledge and understanding of how to gradually build it, but it cannot happen simply by practising this area of work every day. It comes about as a result of the whole work pattern containing the factors which develop collecting work. They are: small circles and lateral work, frequent and well-executed transitions, vigilant use of school and changes of direction. The transitions to and from the variations within the paces must be full of impulsion.

Your half halts ensure that your horse's impulsion is channelled through him to lighten the forehand, never to load it. It is essential that your horse is elastic and yet secure in your rein contact throughout all the changes within the paces.

When you are maintaining roundness, lift and rhythm around the large circle, move off the centre school circles onto the inner track of the long side in your medium strides. Keep them, if possible, for five or six strides and then curve away into a circle line once more as you ask for the strides to return to the working pace. This type of build-up will help you to avoid riding lengthened paces, which dive onto the forehand – many riders fall into this trap. These riders catapult their horses onto the long side of the school in an attempt to practise the test requirement, rather than athletically building the work.

The secret, then, is to mix and match all the ingredients of your work, so that each will benefit the other as you make steady progress.

In the walk continue to concentrate on collection by asking for just a few shorter steps around an eight to ten-metre circle. Be aware of asking the hind legs to come under as you use repeated half halts. Look for a feeling of lightness and a slight shortening of the entire frame. The steps must remain positive and regular when you count the footfalls. Continue to work the exercise where you ask for a mini pirouette. This gives you the added practice of making a bend and displacing the forehand slightly, in conjunction with the practice of riding the shortened steps within an exercise.

The Rein Back

Now it is time to cash in on the work that you have been doing in hand. Change the position in which you have been walking, so that you have your inside arm stretched across to hold the reins lightly, with the back of your hand uppermost and the middle fingers separating the reins. You should walk as before with your horse well forward and yourself by his shoulder. After following your practised pattern of being at the shoulder to indicate forward, and in front of him and facing him to halt, remain in the halt position. Your free hand, as you face him, is now to the inside of the school. Give

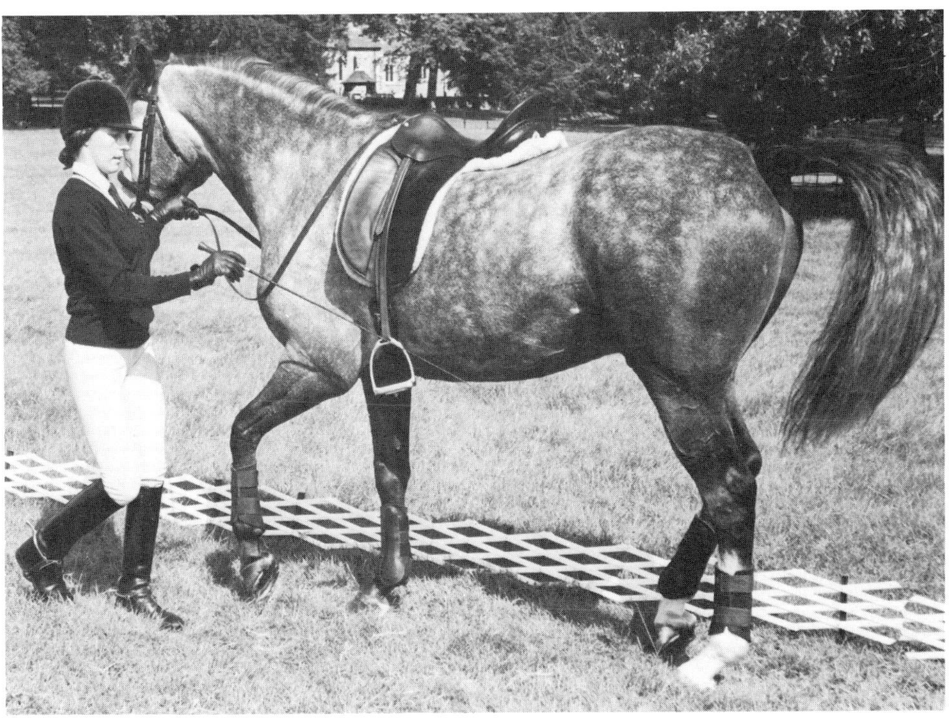

Fig 94 The rein back lesson in hand. The rein contact is constant, the rein aid minimal. Voice, body position and quiet use of whip combine to ask for two or three straight steps backwards.

the command 'back', and press with your free hand (which might be carrying your whip) against his chest or inside shoulder for emphasis. Use very little rein aid, simply maintain the reins in contact lightly. Repeat the entire aid until he steps back one or two steps and then say 'good' and move to your side position with the command 'walk on'.

Repeat the whole exercise of walking, halting and stepping back several times. If your horse attempts to step inwards to avoid straightness, move yourself to the inside slightly and lay the whip flat against his shoulder and rib-cage as a deterrent. Some horses will accept a very light aid with the whip on the quarters to warn the inside hind leg to remain straight. Whatever correction you make, do so quietly, with the minimum of commands. The verbal aids need only be 'back', 'good' and 'no'. Insist on a good clean halt each time before you commence, and make the word 'back' do most of the work for you.

Only work your horse through the exercise three or four times in any one riding session, at a point in the lesson when you have a break. Mount up again to continue with more work, having praised him well. Slot this exercise into your lessons no more than three times a week and ensure that all your ridden halts are positively forward thinking. Anticipation creeps in very quickly. However, the moment he is obviously grasping the

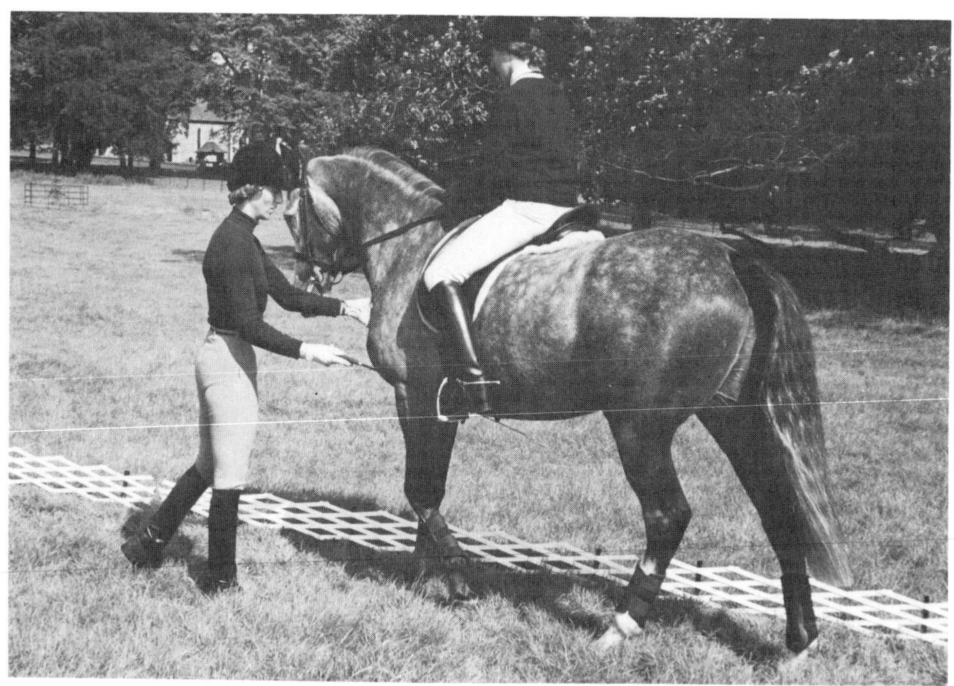

Fig 95 Help from the ground. The rider sits light and begins to apply the legs slightly further back whilst still using the word 'back' as the principal aid.

message from the ground it is time to try the exercise mounted.

Ask a friend to help, by standing in front as you have previously done, but give the verbal command yourself. Take care not to lean backwards; it is better to lighten your seat at this stage. Take your legs just a little behind the girth as you give the command. This serves to make the aid for 'back' clearly different from 'halt' and 'forward'. This will be influential in the future when you require a combination of an exact number of steps backwards and forwards, for the high level tests. As always your aids must relate to the present, whilst slotting into a long-term progress plan.

After one or two steps back, move forwards in a good medium walk. Your rein aids throughout should be giving a closed but not blocking aid. Your hands must always be in front of you and must not move backwards. This is because your horse should answer the lightest of rein aids; he should step back from the aid from your legs because he has halted well, with the hind legs well underneath himself, and the forehand potentially mobile.

Be patient at this stage and you will develop a good rein back. With many horses it is necessary to repeat the aids quietly but firmly for several moments before there is the desired reaction. The mounted rein back training, as with the early in hand work, should be worked during a walking phase, at most three

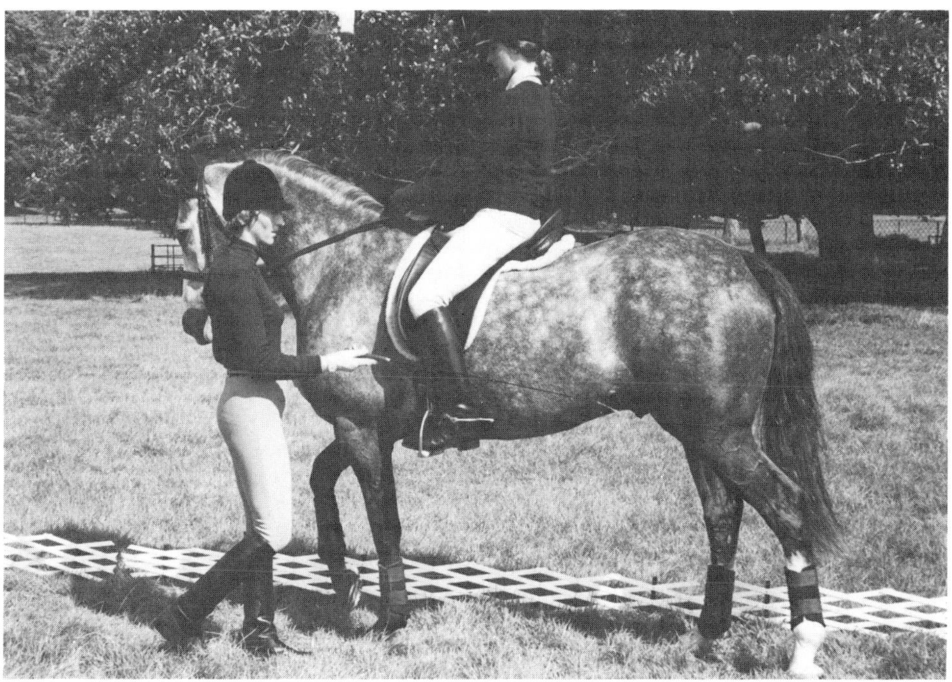

Fig 96 The rider is more upright and the aids are beginning to take over from the voice. I assist less, aiding straightness only.

Fig 97 The square halt. The horse is attentive and on the aids.

Fig 98 Both the rider's legs are drawn slightly back to indicate steps backwards.

Fig 99 The Ditton commences rein back, lifing his right diagonal pair.

Fig 100 With his weight on the right diagonal pair, he prepares for the second step with the left diagonal pair.

Fig 101 Ditton starts the third step of rein back. He is without tension and shows no resistance in his topline throughout.

times per lesson, two or three times per week. If there are indications when you ask for your halts during your work, that he is 'thinking backwards' then leave the rein back until the transitions to and from the halt are forward thinking.

It should be clear from this build-up plan that the ground work is essential and that the horse's learning period must never be hurried in an intensive, shortened burst of training. This plan will pay off. The rein back can be so easily ruined and is rarely retrievable from such a state.

Counter Canter

Your work in the counter canter from the well-balanced return to the track should make regular and continual progress. Provided that your positioning is clear, the upper body being slightly towards the leading leg and legs closely in their individual positions for the specified canter, you will find that you can progressively add more strides along the side of your school or field. Horses who possess a well-balanced canter will soon be capable of maintaining the canter through rounded off corners, to make the short side of the school akin to a big half circle. Keep yourself central, by stretching down well through your inside leg (which is now on the outside of your school, but is still the inside leg to your work). Your outside leg must not overwork, but should simply indicate that you wish to keep the canter lead which you already have. An overstrong, taken back outside leg, pushes the quarters crooked.

Horses who try to break to trot, and quickly offer the inside lead again, have probably been asked too often for the exercise of changing the canter lead through a few strides of trot. It is an exercise which causes anticipation very quickly, and therefore should not be practised too frequently. Progress sensibly, maintaining the counter canter on each rein. Attempt a shallow loop of true canter from the counter canter when balance and confidence in the work increases. It should also be possible to work in the counter canter and then maintain the pace through an easy flowing change of rein back on to its original true canter rein.

Work these exercises evenly on both reins, taking your guidelines of how much to ask from the weaker rein, so that you keep an even progression on both reins.

The learning and consolidation timing for all of these exercises varies a great deal from horse to horse. You must be guided by the improvement generally in the pace and by the obvious ease or difficulty which your horse shows as you ask more of it. Once more, remember that it is the variation of the exercises which will bring the performance together as a whole in the canter. Do not doggedly keep your horse in the counter canter if he is finding it very hard work. Do a little – change the rein and shorten and lengthen the pace, and then return for another short attempt at the difficult work.

From the few shortened strides in the canter around a large circle, you should then move on to attempting twelve and ten-metre circles in the canter. This asks that the shortened strides are accurately controlled and show better collection, due to the size of the circle. Try applying your shortening half halts before the second corner of the short side of your school and then ride a ten-metre circle in that corner. A good follow-up to these shorter, active strides is to ask for a few strides of medium canter on the diagonal, on completion of your circle. This is another example of constantly asking one area of work to help another.

Direct Transitions

As the ten-metre circles improve the quality of the collection offered in the canter, you can ask for a direct transition from canter to walk on the small circle. It will be useful to choose the quarter which is in the corner of your school, rather than the open sector of the circle. As you approach this point, ask with your collecting aids, that is, by stretching your legs down and round as if lifting up his middle piece. As the hind legs step under, give a clear aid on the outside rein for walk. Maintain the walk circle as you ask, because the bending aids will help you to ride the collection through to the transition. Riding the entire circle well is at least half of the battle in this exercise. If your preparation over the last few weeks has been thorough, and you ride the final strides of collecting well, the transition will happen at the first attempt.

The direct transition upwards of walk to canter is not difficult. As long as your horse has understood his canter aids from trot, he has been capable of understanding the requirement. Some horses find the co-ordination needed to move from walk to canter easier. If you have not attempted the transition earlier in your work, use the circle line to make the bend and direction clear; keep the walk forward and on the bit, and apply your precise canter aid.

These direct transitions in both directions will further assist your collection in the canter. Asking for the walk to canter transitions accurately, in every possible place in your school or field, is a part of your long-term build-up to the flying changes. We have thought about these in the jumping work and this is a good point to recollect that although the counter canter work is valuable to the canter, and must be shown in elementary and medium level tests to be established, a horse who becomes too clever at counter canter will not deem it necessary to produce a flying change. He becomes so set in his counter canter, that he has great difficulty producing the co-ordination required for the flying change. Keep this particularly in mind if your horse has found the counter canter fairly easy from the beginning, because it is a common trap to work most frequently the areas that we do well.

Travers

Whilst the canter is making such progress, the trot work will in turn be benefiting from this. As your shoulder-in begins to take shape, showing the power and control to maintain some good steps with bend and collection, it is time to progress further in your lateral work.

Travers is your introduction, with the

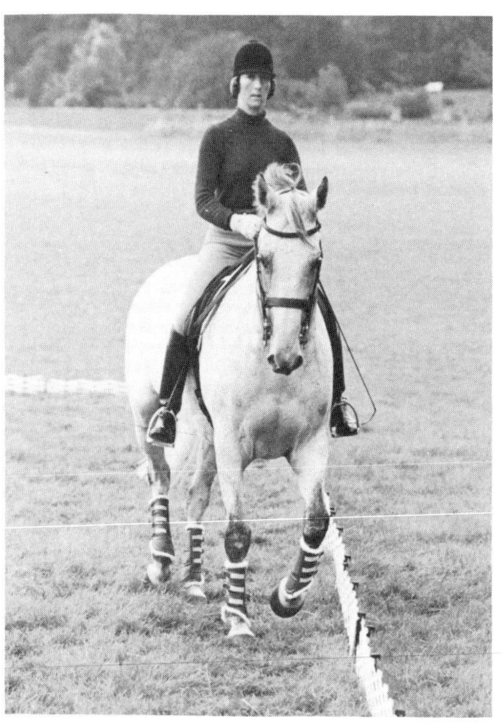

Fig 102 Travers right. The quarters are clearly displaced to the right so that four tracks are seen. The horse is bent to the right through his forehand without loss of control or forward movement through his left shoulder.

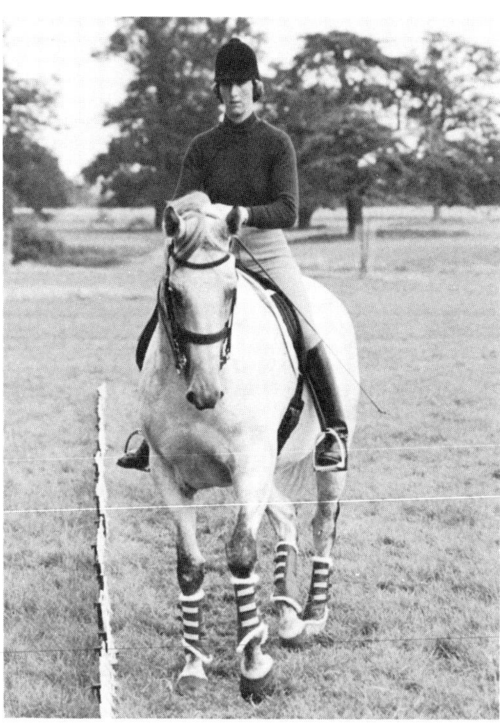

Fig 103 Travers left.

help of the shoulder-in, to the half pass. The contribution of the shoulder-in to the half pass is to bring the inside hind leg more underneath the body to support, to create bend with collection and to bring the shoulders into a position of leadership by way of their displacement from the single track work. The travers displaces the quarters inwards, with the forehand on the track, and causes a bend through the neck and withers to the inside leg. The travers places emphasis on the horse stretching the outer curve of his body and stepping over and forward with his outside hind leg. The collection and bend must be ridden vigilantly asking from the inside leg through to the outside rein.

As in the early days of the shoulder-in, it is valuable to attempt the new exercise in the walk. The easiest way to put your horse into the travers position is to ride a ten-metre circle in the walk, and as the forelegs come to meet the inner track, make a good half halt on the outside rein. This should be done whilst lightly maintaining the forward and bending aid of your inside leg. Retain the outside leg behind the girth and emphasise its effect to prevent the quarters from rejoining the track. The outside leg can make its message clear by being used in a light tapping, repetitive aid at first, possibly with a friendly brush of the whip to see the aid through, once or twice.

After a few steps, and whilst the walk rhythm is still strong, return the hind quarters to the inner track by bringing the outside leg forwards into use at the girth and increasing the inside leg. Do not take the inside leg backwards to do this, its effect must come, as always, from its influence by the girth. Ride this exercise on both reins, always choosing a position to start your circle and travers which allows plenty of strides of straight 'getaway' on your inner track line on completion. Move on to attempting the travers in the collected trot as soon as you are confident, using the same build-up of a circle to lead you into it.

The necessary angle for the travers to exert a realistic influence on the half pass, when it comes into your repertoire, will be four tracks, when you observe it head-on. To begin with, aim for less than this, probably three tracks, as in the shoulder-in. The important point is to keep the bend around your inside leg from the preparatory circle and to keep the feeling

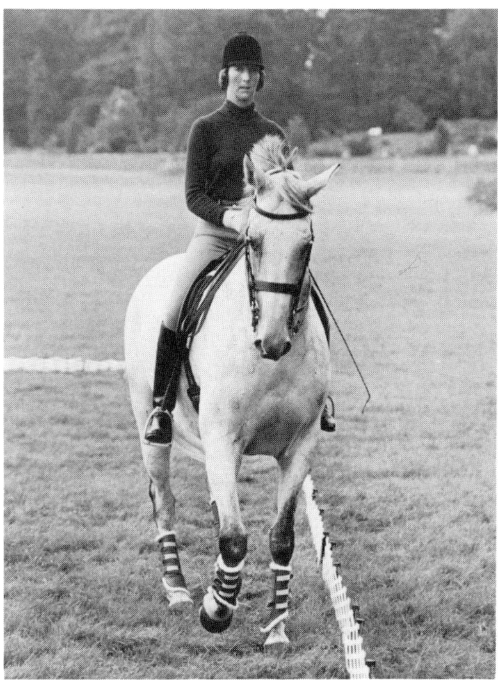

Fig 104 Early work in travers. The displacement of the forehand is less; three tracks can be viewed. This amount of angle is satisfactory for a beginning but will not be sufficient to produce the required suppling effect later.

of impulsion with a little collection coming evenly into both reins. Do not begin the exercise if your horse is uneven in your hands; move away and correct the work through changes of direction and other exercises which you know to be of use.

In the early travers work, your outside leg will be the most important aid, bringing the quarters in for a beginning. As you progress in this work and your horse understands a lighter outside leg to direct the start of the movement, and to place the quarters throughout it, your inside leg once more becomes the most influential, to ride the inside hind leg under and forward, and to retain the important bend throughout. Ride only a few strides in your first attempts; there is more to be gained from a correct entry into the exercise and a well-ridden completion, than from a great number of indifferent strides in the middle. Keep the shoulders forward once again and working, especially the outside one which must stretch forwards and not be allowed to slip outwards to evade the true bend.

Throughout this work and the shoulder-in seek the help of observers to ascertain that you are remaining level in your saddle as you work to create the different influences of leg aids for the lateral movements. It is a good preparatory correction to sit a little to the inside of your horse before you commence, and to stretch your inside leg longer and closer down your horse's side. This serves as an anchor for you and positions your important bending and forward aid to start you off.

Ride plenty of forward working trot exercises alternated with periods of travers so that impulsion is maintained and also take care to work the medium and early extended strides to maintain the balance of this increased quantity of collected and lateral work.

The increase in volume of lateral work is considerable. Do not allow these time-consuming new elements in the work session to rob your horse of his vital loosening-off routine on completion of a section of demanding work, especially at the end of his total work out. The need to stretch those long back muscles is greater than ever through this stage of intensive learning.

Assessing Your Progress

Competitively, you should be producing some very good elementary competition work now. The paces will have improved, making it obvious that he is approaching the next level of work. The tests which demand collection and lateral work will provide you with an opportunity to become confident in your recent work under competition stress. This is good for both you and your horse because he learns to expect much more to be asked of him in the arena.

You will probably have been wearing spurs for some, or most, of your work by now. If your horse has always been very forward-going, however, or over-sensitive to the leg, and this has caused you to avoid spurs, you should begin to wear them now. Use very small spurs with soft rounded shafts if yours is an over-sensitive or ticklish horse. They are obligatory at medium level, so it is wise to have your horse working happily with them, and for you to be adept in the use of them, well before you have the added excitement of longer more demanding tests.

Take any opportunity which arises to ride tests in the sixty by twenty-metre arena. You will enjoy the chance to show the differences in your paces to better advantage and become familiar with the new markers and distances in the long arena. Watch as many different medium level tests as possible. See how the movements slot together and help each other when a capable horse and rider are performing well. Notice how a problem in one movement frequently has an adverse effect on the next, where a horse has a weakness in his work. Observing is also a very good way of learning a test and getting a feel for how it flows, and how it will suit you or pose problems for you and your horse.

By now, you have reached one of the most exciting stages of training, especially if it is the first time you have trained and competed with a horse at the fast approaching medium level. Do your homework meticulously, be brave about your future competition entries, and look forward to the challenge of those large arenas.

8 Medium Level

Taking a Break

At this point both you and your horse may need a short break in the form of a week or two of fun work, hacking or loosening over poles. Horses do not forget work which they have been taught well, but they stiffen up if there are gaps in training where there is no interim suppling work. The principle here is to give him a rest from disciplined learning and freshen him up with exercise which is suppling rather than demanding.

If the local countryside is good, two or three days of walks on a long rein (traffic permitting) involving some hill work, will keep the back muscles working and stretching longitudinally. Follow this up with some working down over poles. Spread your poles in sets of three and five on quarters of large circles around your school or field. Set them out so that you can work over groups of poles at varying distances, for varying lengths of strides, on concentric circles. This means that you can work over poles in a shorter trot, leg yield for a few strides out to a larger circle and work over poles at a longer striding distance. Working him in this way is light-hearted, but it is nevertheless good for his agility, both to negotiate the poles and to use the lateral suppling work in moving between the pole exercises.

Another day or two can revolve mainly around the canter pace, working him in varying lengths of outline, with you off his back, if possible in a jumping saddle to achieve a better balanced position with a shorter length of leg. It is possible to work the different sizes of circles, to shorten and lengthen the canter in this way, yet keep it fun. A horse who is naturally lazy must be asked for lots of forward bursts of longer strides. The keen and nervous type of personality will quietly benefit from a steadier rhythm throughout. Use your common sense to make this fun session also contribute to your horse's work.

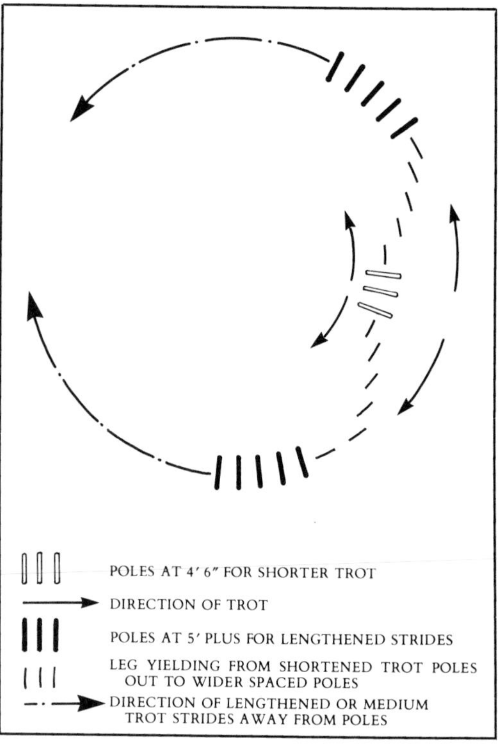

Fig 105 Improving suppleness and agility with trot and canter work over poles.

The opportunity to use the open countryside to have a strong canter is a treat for most horses if their temperament and their canter pace will permit. Once again, you know your own horse so use your discretion. There is no necessity for your horse to fall onto his forehand in this stronger pace. Move away with him in the working canter and build up steadily, keeping him in your rein all the way. Remember to ease off again gradually, and finish with some minutes of round and active working trot with a good rein contact. Loosen off as always with ten or fifteen minutes of walking.

If the time of year and your facilities permit, extra time can be spent in his field here and there during his breather. However, you are not letting him down, so do not allow this on consecutive days; intersperse single days off with light work. After this short interlude, he should come back to tackle his work with an enthusiastic attitude and, hopefully, an appetite for a little more learning. There are still a few movements to be learned before he can achieve a competent medium test.

The Half Pass

Keep the half pass foremost in your mind, particularly its commencement, when the shoulders should be leading the movement with good control. You now have to perfect an accurate and active beginning to the shoulder-in, out of the corner, on the outer track. The agility of the hind quarters, in executing the big steps across which we are aiming for in the half pass, indicates that we now have to come through a deep corner and ask the quarters to come into the travers from the track. They must produce a little more angle than previously, without detracting from the important bend; they must also maintain impulsion with collection in the movement.

In the first part of the requirement there will be no difference in the technical execution of the shoulder-in; your own riding and timing should be effective through a corner and must not lose the activity forward through the shoulders. If the corner riding is forward and accurate and your horse is even in both reins, it is easy to bring the forehand in. This beginning is exactly the same for your half pass.

In the travers, we now have to upgrade from the easy way into it off the circle, to

Fig 106 From a well-balanced corner, straight into left shoulder-in.

a slick beginning off the leg aid. Your horse already knows the exercise, so this is not difficult, simply different. Ride a good, small quarter circle through the corner of the school, in leaving the short side. Maintain the imperative inside leg to prepare for the bend, then ask the quarters to come in with a clear aid from the outside leg applied in the rhythm of the trot. He should not offer canter from the aid, providing that you apply it as previously when riding the travers. It is helpful to keep the outside leg in an asking position through the corner, so that you do not surprise him with a canter type of aid. These are the working preparations; now for the presentation to the new movement.

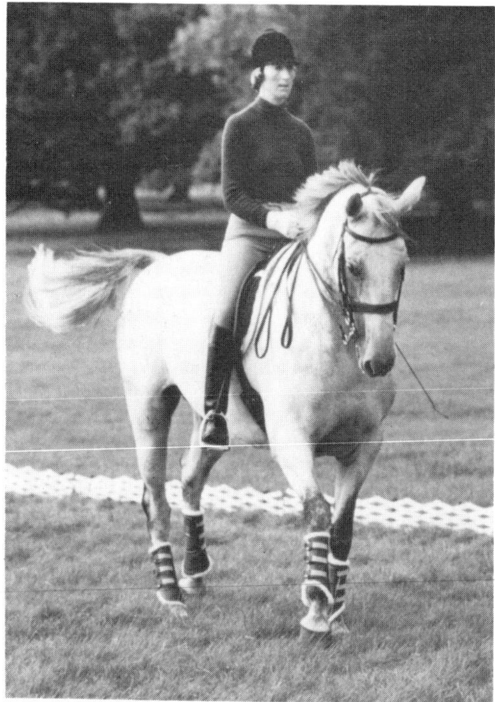

Fig 107 Introducing the half pass in canter. Ditton moves along the diagonal with his shoulders clearly leading into the movement.

I shall lead into the trot half pass build-up as a direct follow-on in your work pattern from the shoulder-in and travers. However, it should be pointed out that if your horse has a better canter pace, you will find it helpful to introduce the half pass to him in his canter work first. Many horses and riders do find the canter easier for the very first introduction to moving laterally into the direction of the bend in the open school. The trot exercises are beneficial to the suppling of your horse whether you begin the half pass introduction in trot or canter; do not omit them if you decide to attempt the canter work first.

In the trot, a very easy way to slip a few steps of half pass into your work is to use the riding of a change of rein on the diagonal line. Do not change the bend for the new direction. This means that you are approaching the new long side of the school with your horse positioned towards it. Keep the bend to this direction, looking at the quarter marker yourself. Half halt on the outside rein and, using the outside leg as for travers, ride him for the last few strides towards the track in half pass position. His quarters will be trailing at this stage. The purpose of this is to utilise the change of direction and the travers which he knows well, to produce an easy introduction to a new direction of movement. Ride this on each rein, from both available directions. He will quickly understand the pattern of the build-up and what you require, because your ground work has been building up over the last few months.

At first you must be satisfied that he moves across with correct positioning of the head and neck, and that you are achieving some crossing. Do not try to attain the bend with the impulsion to move laterally for more than a very few strides. It is better to accept a lesser bend, so long as he is not flattening against the inside bending leg aid. Ride for ease of the movement, initially in a good rhythm, and add lacking ingredients as the movement becomes more accomplished. Your daily build-up to the start of your half pass is important. You must work through your basic foundations and pay much attention to the softness and activity of your shoulder-in and travers. Any stiffness in these two areas of work must be thoroughly ridden through. If it is not, you will start off with a problem in your half pass work.

Your half pass can now be ridden by dissecting the original diagonal line and turning down the centre line to position him for the start of the movement. Once more, start it simply, as if inclining back on one track to the quarter marker, but soon after leaving the centre line make your half halt and ask him into the movement. If you meet resistance, cease going sideways for a stride or two and ride forward, maintaining the bend of the

Fig 108 The Grand Prix horse in the demanding trot half pass required at this level. The horse is clearly looking and bending into the movement to the right, whilst travelling with active hocks and his body parallel to the long sides of the arena.

half pass along your line which is parallel with the long sides. Then, if space permits, half halt and step across again, having had the chance to consolidate how he was feeling towards your leg and rein aids. A long arena makes this particular area of training much easier; for instance, you can ask for a few steps of half pass, then half halt him and ride an active nine or ten-metre circle. From this, you can pick up the half pass with improved bend and collection and move over a few more strides. If space still allows, another break in the movement can be filled with some steps of shoulder-in on the same forward line which you previously rode along with a bend. These are exercises which you must put in regularly to keep the quality, rather than the quantity, of your half passes improving.

Reminders and Corrections

I have stressed the importance of your horse working correctly forward through his shoulders in all his work. If this is not happening you will have a serious problem in the half pass. The control through the corner leading into the movement is vital to a correct and accurate move away from the starting point. Do not, therefore, over-bend the neck laterally and find that, due to this, you have lost the vital outside shoulder to the outside of the bend; it will then be left trailing, rather than leading your horse into the movement. If this happens, reduce the neck bend almost to nothing on the corner, and ride the shoulders over; if necessary, bring your outside leg forward to the girth to assist. Reinstate the bend only when you have the shoulders controlled and working to effect.

You are likely to discover fairly early in this work, as in the shoulder-in and travers, that you have to ride quite differently on each rein, due to your horse's stiff side and softer side showing through. On the soft side you may find his quarters moving into the half pass ahead of your aid, so that he does not allow you to bring the shoulders over in order to lead the movement. Consequently, the quarters lead and the shoulders fall away to the outside. Often the neck appears to be bending well, but in this case the bend has not continued through the whole forehand from your legs. Once more, you must sort him out through the corner which brings you to the starting point and maintain a good inside leg to outside rein connection. In doing so, you keep the inside hind leg under him, from where it works correctly and keeps the impulsion properly forward through the outside shoulder on the turn. In this way you keep both the inside hind leg and the outside shoulder correctly fulfilling their respective roles rather than avoiding their share of the work.

On his stiffer side, your horse will have difficulty in moving through his body with sufficient bend. This will be more noticeable in this movement than in the others which you have tackled to date. He will avoid the bend which you ask by allowing the quarters to trail behind the movement. Your real work for improvement lies in the further suppling of the shoulder-in and especially the travers. Check carefully that he is bending properly around your inside leg, rather than putting the quarters in at a great angle, which can appear impressive but is of no value to the movement without the bend from the inside leg. In the working through of the half pass itself, you must ensure that your half halts keep him as soft as you need him to be in your reins, so that you are able to ride him evenly into both at the outset. In this way, you can correct and ask for more with your outside leg without him running into your hands and setting himself stiffly against you.

At this point you must ride every stride as you wish it to be, with half halts, small circles into the direction of the bend, some shoulder-in steps straight forward and then picking up the half pass again. You will not improve the half pass stiffness by doggedly repeating the exercise indefinitely. On the contrary, the horse can often become stiffer and will be more against his rider as a result of repetition rather than a thoughtful working through of suppling exercises. As always, there must be plenty of forward medium and extended trot worked in amongst your shoulder-in, travers and half passes. You must proceed slowly, so that the good trot half pass develops progressively, as the muscles become more capable due to increased suppleness throughout the body.

The Canter Half Pass

The preparatory exercises for this have already been in evidence for some time in your regular work; they are the shortening and lengthening of your strides and the counter canter. It is useful to add to these some extra work for the shoulders and for mobility through the hind quarters, in much the same forms as in the trot. Work both your working canter and your collected canter with a slight displacement of your horse's shoulders to the inner track. The angle should be very slight. Gain the feeling that you could, from this position, increase the outside leg with your horse even in both your reins and move over for a stride or two towards the centre school. Do the work on each rein, with your counter canter and transitions slotting into the work. Then try a few strides, asking the quarters to work displaced a little towards the inner track. You are aiming here for your horse to be good to your inside leg and remain around it whilst your outside leg just behind the girth asks the quarters to move away from it. He must work straight forward through both shoulders so that the displacement of the quarters works its effect through the whole body.

As always, regulate the speed and the balance with your outside rein. On no account must your horse become strong in this rein, because it is always your controlling and straightening influence which must send its effect right through him. Always use your inside leg at the girth to ask the inside hind leg to come straight under the body once more, and bring the outside leg slightly forward, working your canter straight and on one track. Do not allow your horse to move his quarters to the inside simply because he is crooked; you must have full control of the straightness of the canter before you try this exercise. Do not maintain it for more than five or six strides to begin with, but insist on a good bend and a degree of collection. Move into and out of the exercise from well-applied aids and be accurate: always know where you intend to start and end a movement in your own schooling.

There will be lots of moments in your canter work when you can take a half halt and apply that outside leg aid, asking for a few strides of easy canter half pass; 'easy' because you may have a less than collected canter, with the exercise attempted in a very forward, easy attitude. More specifically you can follow the same thinking as the trot build-up and use the influence of the outer track. Your collected canter is undoubtedly capable of a well-executed turn down the centre line, so make this your beginning and then put your horse in the slight degree of shoulder-fore, which you worked along the outer track in the canter as a preparation. After no more than a step or two of this preparation, increase the outside leg with a clear and, if necessary, tapping aid, whilst your inside leg maintains bend and impulsion. Keep good control of the pace itself. Do not allow your horse to run away from the aid, and see that the rhythm of the canter stays as near to your improved collected pace as you can manage.

From now on you should continue to improve through your suppling work; work on circling within the half pass and sometimes riding forward without sideways steps for a few strides, as in the trot.

The collected canter should now be worked to become very mobile and capable of being ridden around your arena or field with loops or half circles which come within the sizes required in your medium level tests. Ride through large serpentines, maintaining rhythm through your well-timed rein aids. Do not allow your horse to dive onto his outside shoulder through the counter canter curves; this is where your outside rein works again, predominantly with the inside leg, to keep an upright feel in the work. The outside leg assists but should not be too far back or it will work against you by pushing the quarters in. Calculate where you should be touching the side of the arena when working in loops which are not on a clear line between two markers. You will need to develop an eye for this, as it takes much practice to make four to six canter and counter-canter loops through the length of a long arena. You should be more aware of the need for accuracy now than you were six to nine months ago, thanks to your recent work.

The rhythm of the canter should be more established now, in each variation of the pace, and you must continue to differentiate in your own mind which canter you are riding. It is easy to find yourself working in a pace somewhere between working and collected, without it truly being either.

In some of your tests you will be required to show a simple change of the canter lead through the walk. You have done the ground work here through the transitions walk to canter and canter to walk. Obviously, when utilising the ten-metre circles, a degree of the required collection for that more difficult downward transition has been produced by the circle. When you are then required to show this sort of collection along a straight line, perhaps the centre line or on a diagonal, it is much more difficult and requires practice of both the transition and its execution on the line.

Make one or two preparations by collecting the canter on the ten-metre circle and ride the transition coming out of the circle on to the long side. Then proceed to a diagonal line and as you approach X bend your horse and ride into a ten-metre circle. As you are about to complete the circle, collect as much as possible and then ask for the walk. Ride forward in medium walk but do not attempt the upward transition: that transition is not difficult and is easily anticipated, spoiling the movement. Ride this sequence once or twice on each rein, but no more. Achieve the result and then remember to include the canter to walk transitions when the canter shows especially good collection during your work pattern.

Making good canter strike offs from walk and trot, anywhere in your arena or work place, must be kept in mind as part of the work ahead for flying changes. You should now include strike offs into the outside lead to move away in counter canter. Come slightly away from the outside track when you ask for this requirement so that your horse is not inhibited by the outer wall. If your aids are clear and he is well prepared then it will not cause problems.

Improving Rein Back

Your rein back should now have progressed to three or four unhurried and hopefully straight steps back. Previously we were walking forward, both into the exercise and away from it. Now you must begin to put this movement into your other work.

Work in trot and from collection and good preparation, make your two transitions to walk and to halt as active and controlled as possible. When he is not expecting this movement you may find that he does not answer your riding aids as promptly as when they occurred after the build-up which he knew well. Use your verbal aid once more, to quicken his response. Move away from the rein back asking him to show immediate impulsion out of the movement. Very soon he will be ready for the movement to be asked for anywhere in his work.

Be patient on the occasions in the early days when he appears not to have heard your aids at all, as you do not want him to become tense about this important piece of work in the future. When he remains straight in the rein back on each rein, begin to work the movement on the inner track, and later on lines across the school. Continue to progress slowly.

The Walk Demi Pirouette

So far you have shown your horse the shape and direction of this movement, hopefully frequently, but as yet not in a very demanding way. The lateral work in trot has contributed to his ability to show greater elasticity through his body, and this must now be put to use in this movement.

In the demi pirouette your horse must show a turn around the haunches in the collected walk, whereby he maintains four regular footfalls. The hind feet maintain their side by side positioning and must never cross. The outside foreleg crosses over, and in front of, the inside foreleg. The inside hind leg must be replaced as near as possible to the print it left. A very slight forward gain in ground is permissible. The horse is aiming to describe a half circle within his own length and this cannot be done correctly unless his walk rhythm is positive and his walk, as a pace, is highly collected. It is therefore a very difficult movement with bend, collection and much mobility through the whole body, and in particular the shoulders.

The travers work which you have used in the trot and canter is valuable again here. The requirements through your horse's body in all these exercises are the same, but the pace and situation exert a considerable effect on the timing and balance involved. Put your horse in walk on a ten-metre circle and firstly achieve a bold medium walk. Then, maintaining rhythm, shorten the pace and keep the bend around the inside leg. Move the quarters to the inside of the circle whilst paying great attention to the line of the circle along which the forehand must continue to move accurately. Maintain this for four or five strides and ask the hind legs to come straight once more. Do this on both reins to give you the improved feeling of collection and to experience how easily the shoulders drift out. This happens because there is a great deal of stretch asked for, through the outside of the horse, to achieve this positioning on the circle.

Alternate forward thinking trot and canter with this tighter work. Move away from the exercise on the circle and choose a line on an inner track or through the centre of the school. Collect the walk and bend your horse through the head and neck slightly to the direction in which you intend to use the forehand. Keep the inside leg at the girth and use it lightly to maintain the active steps of the inside hind leg. Turn your body and, looking the way in which you are turning, increase the outside leg aid which you must position to the girth, if you know that the movement of the shoulders requires assistance. Position the outside leg aid back slightly if you have an inkling that the quarters will escape on the bend which you are attempting. You should know your horse well enough now to be fairly sure of his reactions and difficulties.

Your hands must both lead the horse round into the demi pirouette, the walk being short enough from good preparation for your horse to make several rhythmical steps around. Do not struggle to complete 180 degrees; if you achieve two good steps, walk forward out of the exercise and then pick another starting point and begin again. The use of the half halts to lighten the walk and lead the horse – already light and mobile in his way of moving – into the pirouette is essential. If your horse is heavy in front, the shoulders are loaded and he will not be capable of making a good start, let alone maintaining it through three or four steps.

However many steps you decide on, make a good controlled exit from the movement so that your inside leg and outside rein work together again to say 'enough' and 'forward'. Progress slowly and ask someone to keep a watchful eye on you regularly, to tell you what the hind legs are getting up to. This is extremely important; once the influential inside hind leg has developed the habit of sticking to the ground, the movement is valueless, as the walk has lost its four time beat. In training vary the pace in which you ride away from the exercise: sometimes in medium walk; occasionally strike off into the new lead in collected canter; sometimes straighten up and trot away. In your medium level tests you will frequently be remaining in walk, so you must be certain that you can produce a calm, balanced walk out of the pirouette when needed.

You now have work within the walk to interchange with your other, more energetic, training. Make it work for you by breaking up each specific exercise of the walk into segments which the other work – canter or trot – can influence with their impulsion.

Fig 109 The start of the demi pirouette, with the horse in collected walk, at the moment of applying the aids to bring the forehand away from the track. He must be even and light in both reins, with the shoulders feeling mobile and upright.

Fig 110 A half halt on the left rein and the rider's body begins to turn into the direction of the movement. The rider's inside (right) leg maintains the walk steps, whilst the outside leg is fractionally behind the girth to discourage the left hind leg from swinging away to the left.

Consolidating Medium Level

You must experiment with the order of working your exercises. You will know well how early in his work your horse needs some canter, or whether he requires the counter canter as further suppling before he works through his shoulder-in, and so on. The medium and extended paces must follow the circling and lateral work to give them the power which they require. The canter half pass may help that movement in its trot, and the walk pirouette work can be of benefit before that phase of work.

Don't be afraid to alter your programme and experiment to find a better or less tiring work pattern. There is a reasonable quantity of work now to be consolidated, so you must select work which you wish to concentrate upon during a work out. It is not necessary to attempt every possible movement every day. Some days of the week should be less strenuous, with either hacking or pole work for fun and relaxation.

When you begin to compete in your medium level classes and your competition schedule is busy, you must ease off the intensity of your horse's training. If you do not, he will lose his appetite for

Fig 111 A slight loss of balance is shown at this stage. With a horse who is new to the exercise it would be wise to step forward out of the exercise if this occurs. Here we shall half halt to rebalance and continue.

Fig 112 The rider's outside leg here is nearer to the girth, to assist in moving the rib-cage area and left shoulder towards the last two steps of the movement. The bend through head and neck is well maintained.

his work, due to travel tiredness and the busy and demanding nature of his recent work schedule.

Introducing the Double Bridle

At some point in the elementary and medium training span, when your horse has achieved a way of going which has given him a confident, secure manner of taking the bridle forward, you should introduce the double bridle. This means finding bits which fit well in his mouth and will produce the necessary effect. By this I mean that if he has a very light, soft mouth and needs persuading to take the bridle, you must choose a bridoon which is of a thick eggbutt type and not one which is light in weight. Likewise, choose a curb bit with short upper and lower cheeks, so that it does not have a great curb effect when the reins are maintained on a light contact (*see* Chapter 5 for further details on types of bit).

Fit the bridle carefully and be sure that it is not tight or pinching anywhere. Look inside the mouth and see that when you take up a contact on the bridoon reins, and also very lightly on the curb, the bridoon bit lies just above the curb in the mouth. Show him the use of the extra curb rein whilst in the stable, so that he feels the curb chain in use gently. There is no need to rush him out into your schooling area to try the double bridle. Quietly go out into the countryside for a hack, where you will simply ride off the bridoon rein as if your snaffle were there

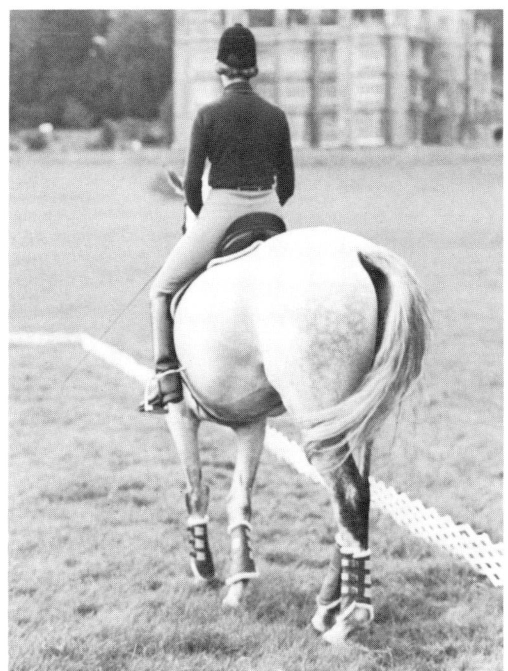

Fig 113 As we finish the demi pirouette it can be clearly seen that Ditton has stepped forward and defined a circle with his hind legs. In the learning stages this is a good idea, to ensure that the walk sequence is maintained throughout the movement.

instead. Do this on several occasions, quite nonchalantly, to accustom him to the two bits in his mouth. He will not be required to wear his double in competition until he is competing in advanced classes, but it is a mistake to leave the change until the horse is well into medium; he may take umbrage at the changing of an item as regular and guaranteed as the snaffle bit. Simply introduce the double bridle gently, at some stage in the second year of training when you feel he is ready for it.

Resting

Finally, when you know that the lessons are being understood and overall, steady progress is promising, give yourself a break and allow him a few days of undisciplined suppling work, so that he remains fresh and happy in his work through these busy and vital months of learning. All work and no play rarely produces a competition horse who is exciting to watch.

9 Flying Changes

The rider approaching flying changes for the first time often feels the inclination to panic. If this happens on a horse who is also totally uninitiated, there is bound to be chaos. This situation can be avoided.

As the rider, you must understand how to ride changes effectively and, if necessary, tactfully on a well-trained schoolmaster. You need a trainer who knows the schoolmaster well, to show you the aids, their timing and their effect. It is vital that you know how to accomplish the changes yourself, before proceeding to teach your horse.

The Rider's Work

This is where your straightness in the saddle is vital. If your seat is slipping sideways, to the outside of the horse, you are never in the middle of him to apply clear, well-timed changes of aids. If this is the case, you should present yourself for your lessons on riding the changes having already worked yourself through a few lunge lessons.

As you watch the single flying changes being ridden, notice these details:

1. The canter is forward but collected.
2. There is no change in speed or rhythm as the horse executes a clean, active flying change.
3. You do not throw yourself from one side of the saddle to the other, in applying the aid. Some horses do tolerate riders who throw their weight around the saddle, and somehow they learn to discern the masked aid underneath. This is not necessary. The horse can be taught with unobtrusive aids, to change obediently from, for example, canter right to canter left.

When you ride the schoolmaster you will realise that you must be positive and decisive, especially with the change aids. You will begin the changes work by riding the collected canter on an easily defined shape such as a ten-metre half circle, with a return to the track. Whilst on the straight line, just prior to the track, you will prepare to change. Don't hesitate over the pass word and make sure that your horse is light and responsive to the present outside rein because you are about to straighten him with it. Bring the new outside leg back behind the girth in a clear brushing leg aid; simultaneously, move the new inside leg into the girth position, to ensure the straightness of the change stride. Your new inside hand must never pull on the inside rein or be restrictive in any way; if this does happen the movement of the inside hind leg forward and under is blocked, and the change may be subsequently short in stride, or late by one stride behind.

You must continue to think and ride forward during the strides after the change. This is very much akin to the landing side of a fence when jumping. When you have ridden changes in both directions, with good co-ordination and timing, you will grasp the importance of using the half halts to balance the canter in the preparation; then, however, you should ride forward into the changes without restriction. The changes will move you in the saddle; allow this to happen and do not go ahead of the movement with your body. Give the aid and wait for the change. You then need to gain the confidence to make changes from counter canter to true inside lead, and to ride more than one change on the long side of the school and finally on the diagonals. By this stage you must be adept enough with the change aids to have sufficient concentration left for riding the straight line accurately too.

Working with Your Horse

The decision to commence work on changes with your horse will not simply depend on his stage of training. The prerequisite is a good quality, nicely balanced canter, whatever the age of your horse. Hopefully you will have been encouraging changes from your young horse earlier in his training. If he has given you random changes when jumping, shying or because you applied a corrective leg aid, you should have praised him, even when the change was totally unrequested.

To begin with, your horse must be capable of moving off from a clear canter aid applied anywhere in your school, from walk and trot. When these seeds are sown, your objective is to make him think of changes by building up his capacity to anticipate. There are several places in the school where you can work the exercise of changing the canter lead through trot. For example, you can proceed in a bold collected canter and make a fifteen-metre half circle near the end of the long side of the school, then incline back to the track. The trot is asked for on the straight line and the strike off onto the new lead just before the track. The shape can then be repeated the other way from this position. Ride the exercise from each long side of the school, insisting that your horse is quick off your aids in all the transitions. Do not over-collect the canter or ride too carefully. An attacking attitude is necessary!

Some horses in the early build-up will begin to show signs of wanting to get into the new canter lead without the trot in the middle. Seize this opportunity if it presents itself, by applying your change aids clearly for the new canter. If a change does not result, repeat the leg aids with a tapping type of emphasis from the outside leg. The whip can be carried on the inside to the new canter, so that you can emphasise the change aid with your whip behind the new inside leg. Even if you find yourself repeating these aids calmly but methodically for several strides, pursue them; if your horse is not quite sure he will take a few strides to work out how to co-ordinate himself into the new canter. If the change happens, walk for a few moments, praising him continuously.

If the change does not happen, continue to ask for it a few more times on each rein. If there is still no change, do not punish him, but rest a moment and think about your own position and the clarity of your aids before you try a build-up in a different place. It is not unusual to need to attempt the first change from different parts of the school. Do not become despondent if your first one or two lessons in this area of work are unsuccessful.

Some horses get the message quicker if ridden on a twenty-metre circle in counter canter at one end of the school and

Fig 114 Falcon returns to the track in a well-balanced canter right. The aids keep him clearly positioned to the inside (right) bend.

Fig 115 On reaching the track, the head and neck are straight, in readiness for the change to the left.

Fig 116 The aid for left canter is applied; the left leg is now at the girth for straightness and the right leg is behind the girth.

Fig 117 Moving forward in the canter left, with the horse soft in the reins and attentive for the next aid.

then asked for a change to the inside of the circle. As in the early training, where a part of the circle was found to assist achievement of the correct canter lead, use the point where a wall or fence necessitates the change to the inside. Have your whip once again on the inside of the circle so that continued taps on the inside, as you move the new outside leg back, emphasise the aid. If you feel that you are on the brink of achieving the change, a sharper tap may make the horse cross for a moment, causing him to kick at the whip and, in so doing, to change.

Use your knowledge of your horse's temperament to guide you in whether the use of whip is pertinent or not. You must never create a situation where your horse is so tense and worried by the exercise which is developing that he cannot canter properly or listen to your aids.

Another area of the school which helps some horses to change is a point at the beginning of the long side. This may, at first, seem strange, but when horses are loose schooled in a *manège*, they frequently change from the inside lead to the outside one on completing the corner and rebalancing themselves in readiness for the long side ahead. You will therefore approach this build-up in the short side of the school, on to the inner track of the long side. Be quick to ask your horse, as he comes off the corner, to go towards the outer track, with a clearly applied aid for the outside lead.

If your horse enjoys jumping, use cleverly placed poles on the ground, or cavalletti, to induce a change over. Most of all, be persistent but patient. Some horses take several weeks of different build-up exercises and use of poles before they begin to give spasmodic attempts at changes in both directions. You can help your horse by working him from his less supple canter towards the rein he prefers, so that the idea of what you would like is coupled with his natural inclination or preference for a leading leg. Interchange this with other canter work, especially that of the half pass. Do not remain working in the canter for a long period without a trot or a break in between. If you do, he will become tired and then you will never get the message through.

Horses who are agile in their canter and have used a flying change in their youth to shy or escape a question are usually easy to teach. Sometimes they are too quick and accelerate away too much, either before they change or after it. This may begin as a fun element, but he should be ridden firmly and calmly to insist that the change is from your aid and not ahead of you.

Do not work this piece of your training in every lesson; two or three times a week is sufficient. Do plenty of work to maintain the even quality and calmness of the canter pace on the days when you miss out the changes work.

Consolidating the Changes

Initially you should ensure that the changes are clean, that is, showing a full and proper stride of canter, but other than this important priority, it is the idea of the change that you are imparting to your horse. When the changes are coming off your aid from the build-up shape, it is time to ask for changes along the straight lines, without the lead-in work.

Again, make use of habit or anticipation. The first changes on the long side of the arena can be easily achieved by riding the long side in a good forward counter canter and asking for a change to the inside a few strides before the corner. Do not over-collect the counter canter stride; your horse is capable of maintaining that counter canter through the corner. By riding a shade stronger towards the change you make it a natural course of action. When this is going well, you will find that he is on the aid quite securely and is enjoying the changes as much as you are. Changes on diagonal lines, over the centre line and on slightly curved lines will come into the pattern of things fluently. At this stage your aid should be quiet and effective so that he looks as if he has a natural ability to accomplish flying changes.

Straightness and Quality

You must now pay more attention to the straightness and quality of each change. If he began them somewhat flamboyantly – swinging his quarters – you must now use your straightening aids of inside leg to outside rein during the change. The rider's inside leg must be used beside the girth throughout the changes to keep the inside hind leg underneath, with the hock bending, as it comes through. By deterring the inside hind leg from moving to the side, we are making it carry weight; its original tendency to move to the side will continue to require thoughtful riding through into the tempo changes in the future.

In riding for quality in the changes, with tempo changes now your goal, controlled balance and straightness through the shoulders is vital to future training. You must be vigilant in maintaining suppleness through both sides of his body in the collected canter, so that he is even in your reins throughout the changes. If he is not even, this will be clear in the changes themselves and in the outline or freedom of the work. Pay attention to the balance of the canter after the change, so you are aware of what is necessary to add another change five or six strides on.

There should be a period of settling down for the changes now. How much work you see through with them in the early stages is usually influenced by your competition commitments and the time of year in which you have chosen to tackle this work. The end of a competition season, after your horse's short holiday, is ideal, mainly because you will disturb his canter work for a while and when you ride the inclines towards the track he will be concentrating on changes because you have encouraged him to do so. It is not possible to pursue this change work *and* expect obedient tests from him.

Correcting Problems

It is essential to have help from the ground, so that you know how the changes look, and why they may not be good enough. From your own point of view, your straightness in the saddle and the way you are applying aids must be monitored so that you do not slip into habits which then inhibit the changes.

Late behind When your horse makes a change and you are told that he was late behind, this means that the hind leg did not come through with the stride of the foreleg, even though the length of step which the hind leg made was acceptable. The rider must always check that his preparation was good enough in keeping the canter round and active. If the hind leg is persistently lazy in rhythm, then the change will improve from riding

Fig 118 Dr Reine Klimke with Ahleric executing the one-time changes during a display at Wembley.

several strides of demanding half pass, to force the late leg in to the position of outside leg to the movement. This is followed by a good straightening up aid, and the aid for the change a stride or two later. Don't let this sort of habit become established.

Late in front If the horse is late in front your corrective work is in improving his quickness and mobility through his shoulders. You must ride the approach to the change, keeping him forward but up through his forehand, never allowing him to convert the forward demand into a dive on to your reins. The last three or four strides, therefore, must be well activated by you so that he gives the feeling of lift and lightness forward through his shoulders before the aid for the change.

Producing Good Changes

Finally, remember that the flying changes are an exciting part of training and learning, and the seeds for good changes can be sown very early in a horse's training. This will enable him to pick up the work and to develop it more easily when the timing is right.

The rider's sense of timing is vital for changes but this must be developed from the feel of a horse who does the work well. A good position and aids, a good schoolmaster and a long-term plan are necessary to produce good changes – with enjoyment!

10 Into Top Level

Now is the time to stand back and look hard at the work which you have done and your achievements so far. Are there any weak links? Are they weaknesses which require immediate remedial attention? Check through the following elements of your work.

Reassessment

The variations of collected, working, medium and extended in the trot and canter paces must be showing clear differences. In the walk your collected, medium and extended walk should be positively marching and show well-defined differences. If there are weaknesses there, evaluate why this is so and decide which exercises will improve those weaknesses. You should also consider whether your training programme has failed to work these elements well enough, and whether a slight change of pattern or priorities should ensue.

Is your lateral work gathering collection and cadence now and is it showing equal ability on both reins? The walk pace should be catching up on collection now too. The pirouettes should have been perfected and the rein back should contain the number of steps which you dictate. The transitions between collected and extended must be feeling and looking powerful, and the return of that variation should have control and straightness. All the canter and counter canter work must be straight showing the variations. Make a plan to do two or three weeks of consolidation work to bring up to scratch the weak points, and then we can look ahead once more.

Top Level Work

Canter to Halt

In the canter, use your collection on the smaller circles to bring you through to the most acute transition – the canter to halt. Reduce the circle to as small as you

Fig 119 Sandy Pleuger Clarke commencing the canter pirouette with her elegant horse, Marco Polo.

can, using a corner, and make the halt as you come off the circle on to the long side. Maintain the halt for several seconds. When the transition is improving, go ahead and try one or two on the centre line. Make the canter as collected as you possibly can, then ask for the halt. You must follow this up with some centre lines ridden with a number of strides of collection, followed by riding forward to working canter, to prevent constant anticipation of halt when you ride that important line.

The lateral work must begin to have a slick, polished beginning and ending to every movement. The half pass can now utilise another exercise to improve it further and to enable you to scotch any indifferent ending to it by riding into renvers.

Renvers

Previously you have used the shoulder-in and the travers as the suppling work to build up to and improve the half pass. This will always be so, but you can now add another exercise which you will begin by working on the track and later, in conjunction with travers and shoulder-in, on the centre line. In the travers you ride the half pass positioning with your horse's forehand on the track. In renvers the hind feet move along the track with the forehand displaced. In both exercises you have the half pass mechanics and bend.

The particular use of the renvers for many horses is that you can pick it up just as you are about to finish your half pass, at the track. This means that you can ride the half pass for a few more strides along the track, so that your horse always realises that he must wait for you to end each movement of half pass and stay on your aids for it.

Imagine that you have turned down the centre line and are riding a half pass in trot (later you will also use the exercise in the canter) towards the half marker. As you reach a point approximately one metre from the track, you will half halt your horse and make the forehand wait as

Fig 120 Falcon in renvers left. He is bent to the left and stretching forward into the movement through the right shoulder. The rider's left leg at the girth maintains the bend and asks the left hind leg to step well under the horse's body to carry weight.

you move the quarters over, into a quarters leading position. With the quarters now on the track, maintain the bend towards the direction in which you are moving and ride forward in the renvers. Your horse must keep looking straight forward down the inner track line. The bend is maintained firmly round your inside leg and your outside leg is controlling the outside of the bend, but is also instrumental in riding the forward impulsion and activity of the outside shoulder. When you wish to finish the movement, you must positively half halt and, returning the forehand crisply to the track, ride forward.

In your shoulder-in you should now use this method of returning the forehand to the track on some occasions to end the movement. The options of how to end any movement must be yours and your horse must always be ready.

The Trot

Your trot work now has many variations of movements to be linked together in different patterns: for example, shoulder-in ten strides, circle eight, nine or ten metres into travers ten strides, straighten and forward in medium trot. This and similar variations can be ridden on the outer track and, when you feel ready, on the centre line. A good half pass improver is to ride half pass from the long side quarter marker to the centre line; at X ride into a collected trot eight-metre circle in the same bend, and complete the circle with the hind legs on the centre line, maintaining the same bend to ride in renvers down the centre line, and return the forehand to the line to finish. There are many more formulae and you must interchange them to achieve the best results for your horse. The principle of mixing medium and extended walk with your more high-powered collected work holds good more than ever.

The Canter

As your changes become more established in the canter, you can use them in your serpentine loops which stretch the full width of the school. The changes over the centre line between the curving lines require your horse to remain upright and well balanced, whether he is approaching the change from his true canter or counter canter. He has to be forward enough through his outside shoulder on the curve which touches the outer track to be positioned ready for a change one or two strides before he strikes the centre line, which is exactly where the change must happen. This requires excellent control and much concentration, because in competition both the changes and the shape and accuracy of the serpentine are being marked. The changes themselves will be required as a test of balance after movements such as extended canter on the diagonal. This is a rider exercise, once the horse is capable of the elements which constitute the movement.

When you first attempt to put together this mixture of requirements in training you must move your diagonal line to give more room to the corner which you are approaching. This is so that the change is not inhibited by the fact that the corner is approaching quickly. Ride for your maximum extensions, but bring your horse back from the extension in good time over a period of several strides. Check your straightness, then position for the change and the long corner line, and boldly ride forward into both. In this way you ride the exercise by breaking it down into pieces, riding each segment well. You will gradually make the quality of the whole movement sharper by producing the degree of pace and expertise required for the test.

There are two more areas of canter work which you must work on or towards in the weeks ahead. Start to join together your half passes and flying changes, so that the counter change of hand in the canter (in its easiest form of half pass–straight–change–half pass) can be put together. Get each section technically correct so that the shoulders are leading the half passes and the changes are straight. When you eventually try to go from the change immediately into the second half pass, you must move the quarters over clearly in the last two strides (later on one stride) of the first half pass. This puts the shoulders into the lead to continue the second half pass out of the change. The build-up exercise is the important part here.

Tempo Changes

Begin to make three flying changes down the long side of your arena. You have probably, for some time, found it easy to make one at the beginning of the long side and another before the end of it. Now count the number of strides between the changes to get yourself into the habit of counting and riding. The counting ultimately has to relate to the number of changes and the number of strides between them; you need to know, for example, that you have completed three of your four time changes and that you have two more to go. When you begin four time tempo changes in two to three months (or less), your counting must be in this vein: *1*234, *2*234, *3*234, *4*234, *5*234. This requires practice, so start thinking it through as you ride the changes with longer numbers of strides between.

Pirouettes

At this stage you should be working on your pirouettes in canter. All the work which you are doing to improve the half passes and your general suppling work contributes to this end. However, you can begin reducing the circles and using the travers and shoulder-in positions as specific exercises.

Use fifteen-metre circles in your collected canter. Put the shoulders a little to the inside, keeping the outside hind leg always accurately describing the circle. When you have worked the shoulder-fore position, move the quarters in on the circle, keeping your horse stretching forward through his shoulders correctly, so that he does not escape the bending influence of the exercise by moving his shoulders to the outside and bringing the neck and head around only. Your outside rein is vital in helping you achieve this result.

These exercises can be built up until you are working them for several good and well-collected strides around a ten-metre circle. As in the walk pirouette build-up, progress consistently, but make sure the quality of the pace is your main priority. The footfalls of each stride must remain clearly three time. In addition to this work, decrease the canter circles to as small as you can comfortably make them, whilst still achieving two or three strides of extreme collection. From these strides, ride smoothly but positively forward away from the exercise. As you do so, maintain the controlling outside aids. These are vital to keep the quarters contained and the hind legs under and in position, so that there is no opportunity for the outside hind leg to swing out and cause the canter rhythm to falter when you move away from the tight circle. These canter exercises are demanding and you must obviously work them only a few times on each rein, before riding some forward canter work, possibly off your horse's back, allowing him to stretch his entire topline within the pace.

Planning Ahead

You now have quite a volume of work in your daily and weekly programmes. Plan well ahead for competitions and make sure you maintain accuracy in your day to day riding. Link movements together as though they were in a test, so that your preparation becomes quicker and your beginnings and endings to all your movements are exciting to watch. Your horse will enjoy all the new lessons which he is learning, but also keep up his enthusiasm by including, as always, lots of recreational days.

Continue to have your homework and competition riding recorded on video, if possible, so that you can analyse it and see where improvements can be made. Always seek to correct and improve your own riding. Ride horses under instruction whenever a good opportunity presents itself, and particularly if you are experiencing a problem in teaching your horse new work. Above all, enjoy your horse and your learning, for he can only perform as well as you can ride him.

Appendix Lunging and Longreining

There are many occasions during the horse's training where lunging is necessary and can be of great value:

1. It is our way of introducing the young horse to early discipline, the aids of voice and whip and of developing his muscles at the start of his lifetime's work.
2. Horses who have become difficult or dangerous to ride can be reminded of these early disciplines on the lunge and can be persuaded to start ridden work once more with an improved attitude.
3. On the lunge, a horse who has carried himself badly, possibly fighting the rider in a hollow outline for a long period of time, can be persuaded to stretch his head and neck forward and down to build a well developed topline.
4. The lunge can be used to discover a horse's way of going and jumping without the rider.
5. When a horse who has a condition in the back or girth region must be kept working without saddle or girth, while it heals, he may be lunged.

Whatever the reason for lunging, it is an excellent opportunity to watch your own horse working; to study his paces as others see him and to consider the way in which he moves through his back – all the things which you generally do not see.

The Young Horse on the Lunge

Lunging is an important stage in a young horse's life and it has a great influence over his work and attitude in the years to come.

Before you start, make sure you have safe, supportive going underfoot. It is better to leave the youngster unworked than to risk his joints and tendons by lunging him on hard or deep going. An area of twenty metres square is ideal and, if you are not fenced in, it is useful to have props such as tall barrels and poles to make some sort of barrier around the lunge area.

Equipment

Good equipment enables you to work with your horse properly and safely. The following are needed in addition to your horse's bridle, saddle, breastplate and leg protection:

1. Lunge cavesson.
2. Lunge line: strong and not slippery, with a good attachment piece. Nylon is not suitable.
3. Side reins, from the bit: strong, supple with strong buckles and trigger clips which release quickly.
4. A well-balanced lunge whip, of good length.

The preliminaries of lunging for the young horse are good handling and leading. I shall assume that he has become accustomed to his bridle and leg protectors and can be fitted with the cavesson and the bridle, minus noseband. Everything must fit snugly. The jowl strap of the cavesson, which is sometimes mistakenly thought to be a throat lash, must fit securely below the large cheek-bones in order to be firm around the horse's face. The cavesson must be firmly fitted, so that it will not slip around when the lunge line is attached to the centre ring. It is the front of the horse's face which you intend to influence from the line so it is sensible to have the side rings removed if they make a lot of noise and are likely to irritate a youngster on the front of his nose.

The lunge line should be approximately seven or eight metres long and of a non slippery material with some substance to it. I use strong webbing which is good to hold and use in the rain. Choose carefully, because a slippery lunge line will make your work difficult or even dangerous. The very end of the line should have a large loop which acts as a safety device should the horse pull away suddenly, but will not become fixed and dangerous around your hand or wrist. Wind the line loop first into the hand from which you are going to lead. The line will hang in its evenly-coiled folds about one third of a metre below your hand. Always keep the line tidy because if a loop drops away and you lower your hand from where it should be you may step in it and find yourself in a dangerous situation.

First Steps

Lead the horse around the area in which he will be worked on each rein. Your whip needs to be carried point down with the lash up into your hand, not trailing, but so that you can give a light tap on the horse's quarters with the shaft of the whip to keep him forward if he attempts to stop or is inactive. Lead him from both sides every day so that he is equally happy to be led from his off side.

At this time he must be taught to take a contact through the lunge line with your hand, because this is what we shall look for in later work on the lunge. Practise halting and walking. Remain by his shoulder and insist that he stays sideways to you and does not turn in to you as he halts. In this way, he is encouraged from the beginning to halt straight and squarely. Commands can be preceded with his name, if it is short, or the word 'and', so that there is always one word which warns him that a command is following. Make your word for halt sound quite different from the command to walk.

If you are new to lunging you may feel more confident having someone to work with you when you first work the horse away from you, onto the circle. In this case, they can assist by standing at a point about two-thirds of the way along the line between you and your horse's head. Your assistant will simply give the horse a guiding hand nearer than yourself, whilst you issue the commands and carry the whip. Personally I always work a young horse on my own, unless he is big or very strong. If that is the case, my assistant holds the line at the centre point of the circle and I work a few metres away, still a good distance from the horse, using the verbal commands and the whip. When the horse has learned to lunge kindly and not use his strength, I can continue single-handed. This may take a matter of weeks.

When beginning on my own I move about with the young horse, with a good contact through the line, gradually moving him away from me in the walk. I use the butt of the whip to indicate quietly that he should move away and walk in order to keep the forward flow. In the first few days of lunging I move him away into trot fairly soon because he is unlikely to walk out and away on to a fifteen-metre circle and remain on a good contact within walk at this point in training. The command for trot is clear if it is 'ter-r-rot'. Use the warning 'and', followed by a click of your tongue and the aid of a quiet whip. He will only require three or four attempts at this to know your meaning.

Your whip should be carried so that it is a continuation of your forearm and hand. Always keep the whip quietly moving along that horizontal line which will stretch forward from behind the hocks to near the girth and shoulder. Behind the hocks the whip indicates that the horse should move forward; pointed at the rib-cage it tells him to bend; and pointed at the shoulder it tells him to move forward and not to fall in on the circle. Your whip is working as your legs would, to create bend and impulsion, and your line is your contact through which you continue the bend and regulate impulsion. Learning to co-ordinate these

Fig 121 Teaching the young mare to move forward straight, taking a positive contact on the lunge line. The horse is Special Edition (by Mastercast).

two influences, plus the effect of your own body position, takes a fair amount of practice and experience.

Your position has a substantial effect on the horse. If you get too far behind a young horse, he can easily spin around and go the other way. When you move too far forward, he will stop and possibly run backwards from you. You must take care to observe the influence your position is having, as this factor is frequently overlooked.

Walk and Trot

Work through walk and trot transitions on both reins. Praise him when transitions are quickly offered. Don't chatter to him; make sure your commands and praise are clear, concise verbal aids. You will need to move in and work closer to him in the walk, especially in the early days, to see that the transition is forward to the walk. Likewise when you ask for the halt, position yourself carefully. Tactfully insist that he remains sideways on to you and does not swing his quarters to the outside in order to turn in and face you. If there is a problem with this, return to walking fairly near to him on a shorter line and firmly persist with voice and the butt of the whip against his shoulder, until he remains straight into the halt. Then you can ease away from him again and continue from a good working distance of approximately eight metres.

In the working trot, it is helpful to move with the young horse, but make sure you do not wander. Make two-thirds of a circle, move a few paces slowly with him and circle there. He must learn over a period of weeks to be capable of working around a twenty-metre circle; this will involve you walking a small circle to do so, because lunge lines are not usually ten metres long. Whether you are working in a school or a field, he must be worked in the different areas and corners, so that they are not totally new sights when you later ride him there.

A young horse who has not yet been ridden will steadily build up his work on the lunge from fifteen minutes at the start of training to twenty-five or thirty-five minutes total, when ready for backing and light riding.

Introducing Saddle and Side Reins

After a few weeks of lunge work with just the bridle and cavesson, you will have introduced the horse to a roller and possibly also to a lightweight saddle

Fig 122 Starting work with the side reins attached and learning to remain straight at the halt, ready to move forward without turning in to me.

without its stirrups and with flaps 'surcingled' down. When he is happy with these and is working down with a good stretching topline on big circles it is time for him to learn about the first contact of side reins.

With a young horse I prefer leather side reins with a strong, short elastic inset which stretches a little. A solid leather side rein with no give is a rather tough beginning. Side reins with an over-elastic stretch to them, however, are inclined to encourage the youngster to give long, rude pulls against the contact, and must also be avoided. Fit the side reins to the girth tabs of the saddle by slotting them in and out of the two tabs in use, to prevent them dropping down from the position in which you set them. They must be positioned approximately halfway down the girth tabs, or slightly lower for a young horse; this is a very approximate guide because saddles are so different.

You must judge the length by the horse's outline whilst standing, and by using your knowledge of his way of stretching without them. Adjust them on the long side to start with; never put them on and then turn him. Always adjust them and lead him forward on to the circle so that he moves forward into them; this is the routine he is familiar with. You do not want him to suddenly feel them and go up against them. This should not happen provided that he has first worked in well without them (this is essential) and that they are fitted long enough.

Take care not to make a sudden movement with your whip until he is accustomed to the feel of the side reins. He should be encouraged forward and down into them; you may find yourself walking more with him now, to keep him thinking forward and learning to accept a contact with his bit. Take the side reins off the bit for his walk work. The side reins can be put back over the withers and clipped to the front 'Ds' of the saddle at this time. When you change direction, unhook the side reins and put them up over the withers so that they do not hang down from the girth, where the trigger clip can hit the legs if the side reins swing. When he works confidently in the side reins in trot, he is ready to benefit from some work in long reins.

Canter Work on the Lunge

Whether or not to canter on the lunge depends on the horse, and is a matter of common sense. If the horse has shown a well-balanced way of moving when he has moved into canter of his own accord, it is a good idea to ask for a few strides and move with him so that you do not pull him around the circle. If he has the opportunity now to answer the word 'can-ter', it will help you when he is ridden; the practice at co-ordination is also beneficial.

The second consideration when deciding whether or not to canter, is the going underfoot. If you are on an arena which is slippery and he skids, you will dash his confidence and he could get hurt. On good going he should canter, but only if there is plenty of space; you should have no problem if he has been well-prepared through his other work. In this lunge canter work, I am referring to horses of four years old or more, with no obvious limb weaknesses.

He must not wear side reins for this pace, as he needs the freedom of his head and neck to help him maintain his balance and the pace. Through these stages of lunging, backing will usually be taking place. Lunging is beneficial for some time after he becomes a ridden horse to keep the work forward thinking and active until the ridden aids take over those responsibilities.

Corrective Lunging

Working a horse on the lunge to attempt to rebuild a weak, hollow or rigidly stiff topline calls for considerable expertise, patience, and excellent management of the horse in question. You may be inclined to ride him and work him down from leg to rein, but there are several reasons why you may find lunging more useful.

If the horse has been roughly ridden for some time his thoughts towards any rider will not be very charitable. He may also have long-term sore back muscles from such a rider. For this horse, a break from saddle and rider are essential to change his thinking and to give you a co-operative beginning to build upon. Another horse who may appreciate being riderless is the one who has had a curb bit pulling his mouth about for a time. This horse will need to be lunged with no bridle for several weeks, and probably without a saddle too, for a complete break from a rider.

With these horses, we have to lunge them working for the stretching down attitude of the young horse. However, these older horses will be fitter and may have lost their natural trot rhythms; they may rush around on the lunge, falling in and losing balance. The canter will not be any better as it is likely to be the most abused pace. Much slowing down and use of the voice, and some very long-term work on the lunge is needed here. You must be extremely patient. If the horse is an ex-jumper, using poles will cause him to rush. If he is not, pole work may be well utilised. When you are getting a slightly softer back after some weeks of lunging, the saddle can be fitted once more.

This type of horse, when he has settled to the lunge, will often benefit enormously from working in a schooling aid called a chambon. The equipment is fitted in such a way that it teaches the horse two facts: when his head is high and his back is hollow, the bit is lifted increasingly higher in his mouth and is uncomfortable; when he lowers his head and neck, the bit sits normally in his mouth and is comfortable. When the chambon is in the hands of a trainer who lunges with good feel for the horse and the work, it can produce excellent results as a means of showing the horse how comfortable it is to work with his back swinging and his topline loose. The horse is worked on the lunge with the chambon loosely fitted. As the work proceeds, the chambon is altered little by little until it is effective enough to show the horse when he is working in trot that it becomes comfortable when he stretches. For this work in the chambon, the trot must be fairly slow; it should encourage the horse to let go of his tight back muscles and let them move freely. The horse's work can be built up to about twenty-five or thirty minutes each day in this exercise. The ideal follow-up is for the horse to be mounted and taken for some walking off discipline on a loose rein.

A total lunge programme for this type of horse who has a great deal of repair work to undergo may be three months or

Fig 123 As William commences work at the trot he is slightly hollow and 'flat' in his way of going.

Fig 124 He now stretches his topline and begins to use his whole body efficiently.

Fig 125 Before . . .

Fig 126 . . . and after.

more in duration. The lunging on the chambon can be worked for three or four days a week, and the horse quietly hacked out by a good rider who will leave him alone on the remaining days.

Longreining

It is a fascinating and exhilarating experience to work both a young horse and a trained horse in the long reins. Let us consider the reasons for choosing to longrein, firstly with a young horse who is in the process of being backed.

When the youngster is backed and working on the lunge with his rider sitting quietly, there is a stage where the aids are still totally in the hands of the trainer in the centre. The new rider has to progress to the stage of applying acceptable, lightweight aids and, within a short space of time, have some steering capacity to begin the ridden work free of the lunge line.

Longreining in walk and in trot is a good means of teaching the young horse about the rein aids. It is also valuable in that the trainer can be directly behind the horse, which means that the horse must move first when he is told to; the trainer's voice will be similar to that of a new rider, coming from behind the horse and not, as it was on the lunge, from a reassuringly visible position. For this reason, young horses who do not go forward happily to take on new situations and surroundings can be longreined, even just in the walk, and can thus be persuaded to be braver about the outside world. The trainer can also work from a position where he is further back than when lunging, but is still on one side of the horse rather than directly behind. In this position, the trainer can drive the horse effectively past objects or surroundings which the lunged horse could avoid by shying away. These are some very practical circumstances which can be dealt with, in addition to teaching the horse with the rein aids to turn and to halt.

It is worth mentioning here that the comparative sizes of you and your horse are more relevant in longreining than in riding; to longrein a 16.2hh. four-year-old if you are not tall or very strong yourself is asking for trouble.

Beginnings

Where equipment is concerned, you will need to use your initiative to make use of the most suitable roller or saddle which you possess. I usually begin with the stirrup irons on the saddle well secured up by the leathers and neatly locked around them. The long reins (or two lunge lines joined together) are then brought through the iron so that they run freely. This is important because it is dangerous if you cannot release a rein quickly when you need to. You will need at least one helping hand to hold your horse while you put the reins on.

Work your horse as usual on the lunge before you move to the longrein work, so that he is not too fresh and has done his basic work. It is best to roll up your long reins tidily and stand near your horse, on the side from which you are going to commence. Pass the ends of each rein forward through its own stirrup to your assistant who attaches it to the bit rings. Thus you avoid having the reins tangled up or in any way dangerous. You will now have one rein coming directly to you, and the rein on the other side of your horse coming through the stirrup and over the top of the saddle to you. From here, with your assistant by your horse's head, you can begin to move the reins, quietly flapping them around him whilst you use your voice to reassure him that all is well. He must become accustomed to the reins touching his side, so you have to move around him whilst at the halt – go behind so that the reins touch each side of his quarters.

I have known some horses who never could come to terms with the long reins at all and would have lost a great deal of confidence if I had insisted that they must learn. They proved to be safe and happy under saddle, but could not cope with the reins on their sides. So take great care, because although some accept the long reins readily, others do not.

If all is well with acceptance of the reins, move back and away a little so that you are opposite his flanks, and ask him to walk on. Work him from this position, walking and halting using the reins very lightly. Throughout this work, it is useful if your assistant is near at hand but not leading or influencing your horse. Do the same work on the other rein, from the equivalent position. This amount of introduction is satisfactory for one day. Follow it up the next day – again always lunging first. Aim to move further away from him and after some walks and halts, try some trot from your lunging position. Do this on both reins and praise him a great deal. You should now be able to move around him with the reins flapping and brushing his sides at the halt.

In the walk you must build his confidence so that you can change direction

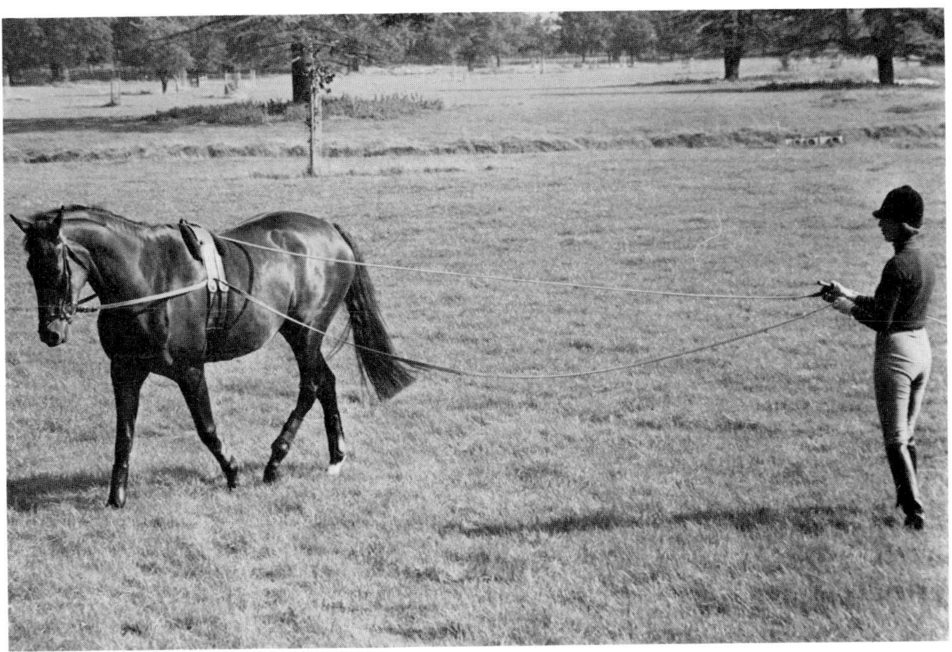

Fig 127 Longreining at the walk from the control lunging position. Here the roller is being used in place of the saddle.

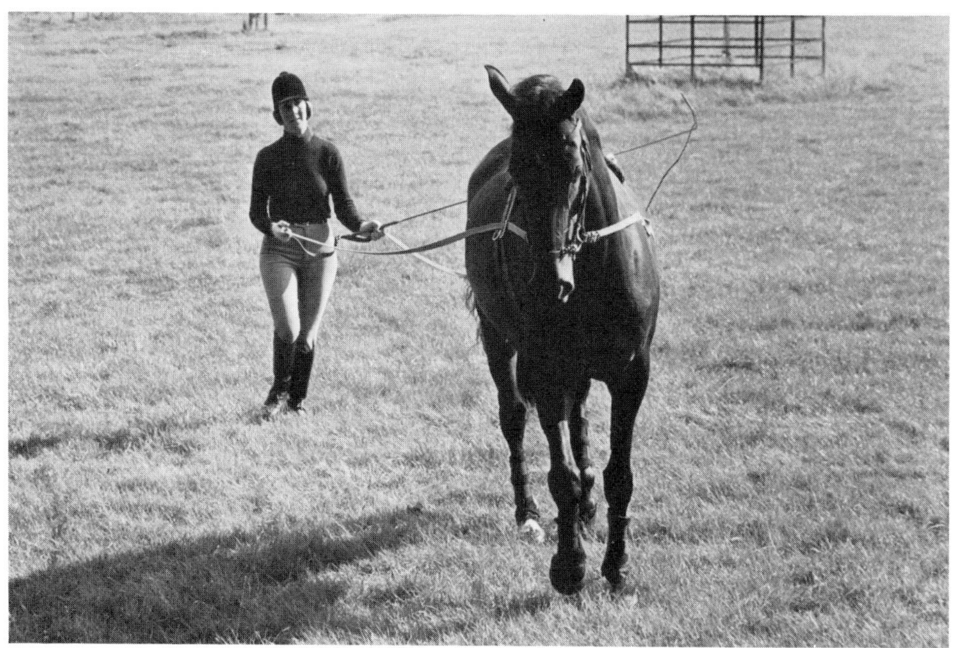

Fig 128 Teaching Special Edition to be brave and walk out, irrespective of whether she can see me or not. At this point she is also learning to accept the left rein coming across her quarters.

Fig 129 Working confidently out in the open in the long reins.

Fig 130 Caruso working his Piaffe *in the long reins; both hind legs can be activated whilst straightness is maintained.*

Fig 131 Caruso, an ex-Grand Prix competitor, is kept active without carrying rider weight, in the long reins.

Fig 132 A great partnership – aim high!

easily on the move, by going behind him and lifting the reins well clear on the cantle as you move across. From here, be a little more ambitious each day, until you can efficiently drive him from behind with a very light contact, or work from a lunge position with one rein coming over the saddle to you.

All this work takes extra time and effort, but if well done it can make your horse much more confident in addition to giving you a better, softer reaction to the reins when you give your first ridden aids with them. Do remember, though, that it is essential to have help at hand when you first attempt to introduce long reins to the youngster.

Training

I use longreining with the horse who is already trained to medium level and above mainly to enjoy the feel of working a horse from the ground in closer partnership than that which lunging produces. In horses who have become very heavy and loaded on their forehands, longreining can encourage lightness and an improved reaction to the rein aids. I never use this method of training on a horse who, through conformation or manner of going into the bridle, would easily overbend. This is because I do not have the legs to assist in making the vital half halts; longreining, however well co-ordinated between rein, whip and body position on the ground, can give many horses the chance to become strong in the rein whilst losing length of neck.

In the training of the horse for *Piaffe*, long reins offer the golden opportunity to have him absolutely straight and to stand in the only position where either or both hind legs can be asked to work harder. Once more, this is work for the expert trainer because the use of reins and whip have to be finely co-ordinated. If you are a beginner, seek out the opportunity to learn how to use the long reins on a horse who can give you some basic experience; he may be a ride and drive cob who is comfortable in long reins, or simply a horse of about 15.2hh., with round rather than extravagant paces, who will patiently allow you to experiment.

If you ever have the opportunity to be shown how to longrein an advanced dressage horse, you will see the trainer working in close to the horse, very near his quarters, to achieve lateral work. It will become even more obvious in this situation of advanced longreining that feel, co-ordination and the positioning of the rider's body, can produce a very close partnership. When that horse and rider have worked together through a sound ridden system of training, to a high level, and they progress to showing their work on the long reins, it is indeed a dressage partnership.

Useful Addresses

The British Horse Society
British Equestrian Centre
Stoneleigh
Kenilworth
Warwickshire
CV8 2LR

Equestrian Federation Australia
Incorporated
Federal Secretariat
2nd Floor
77 King William Road
North Adelaide
South Australia
50006

The Hunters Improvement and National
Light Horse Breeding Society
Mr G. W. Evans
96 High Street
Edenbridge, Kent

New Zealand Horse Society
Incorporated
P O Box 1046
Hastings
Hawkes Bay
New Zealand

USA General Interest

American Horse Council
1700 K Street, N.W., Suite 300
Washington D.C. 20006

National 4-H Council
7100 Connecticut Avenue
Chevy Chase, MD 20815

Horsemanship Safety Association
5304 Reeve Road
Mazomanie, WI 53560

United States Pony Clubs
329 South High Street
West Chester, PA 19382

USA Show and Sport Organisations

American Grandprix Association
Valley Forge Military Academy
& Junior College
Wayne, PA 19087

American Horse Shows Association
220 East 42nd Street/4th Floor
New York, NY 10017

National Horse Show Association
of America
35 Sutton Place
New York, NY 10022

United Professional Horsemen's
Association
181 North Mill Street
Lexington, KY 40507

Professional Horsemen's Association
of America
S. Lake Street, RR 2, Box 93
Litchfield, CT 06776

United States Combined Training
Association
292 Bridge Street
South Hamilton, MA 01982

Index

Additives 49
Aids 57;
basic 62–6;
braking 66;
in flying changes 130–1;
leg 64–5;
rein 65–6, 109;
straightening 96;
verbal 56, 64, 108, 109
Alexander Technique 9
Arena 55–6, 78
Athletic jumping 89
Azoturia 50

Back 50;
and stomach treatment 46;
strengthening the 88–91
Balance 62;
loss of 65–6, 68
Bandages 77, 83–6;
thermal 86
Base 7, 11, 60, 69;
strengthening the 87–9
Bend, in the half pass 122–3
Bit 79–81;
sitting behind the 68
Blood tests 52
Boots 77, 83–6
Breastplate 56, 83
Breathing 45, 46
Bridle 56, 57, 79–82;
double 81–2, 128–9
Bridoon 81, 128
Browband 82

Canter 137, 139–40;
extended and collected 92, 94–6;
half pass 123–5;
in flying changes 130–4;
lead 70, 72;
medium 105–6;
on the lunge 146–7;
to halt 137–8;
working 24, 69–72
Cavalletti 134
Cavesson 79
Chambon 147
Chiropractor 50–1
Circles 55, 72, 77, 87–8, 95, 96, 97, 137–8
Collection 91–6
Commands
verbal 98, 143–4
Competition 73–86;
administration 75;
entries 73–5;
newcomer to 73, 75;
preparation 73–6;
prospects 26;
venue 73, 75
Conformation 19, 20
Corridor (between legs and reins) 65, 66, 72
Counter canter 95, 112–4
Curb 128, 147
Cycling 44

Demi pirouette 26;
in walk 96–7, 125–6
Dentist 50
Dress 77

Education (of the young horse) 56–7
Equipment 75–6, 79–86;
for lunging 142–3
Exercise
horse 48–54;
rider 44–7
Extension 91–6, 104–7

Faradism 50
Feeding 49

Fitness
  horse 48–54;
  rider 43–7
Flying changes 130–6, 140;
  build-up to 114;
  consolidating the 134–6
Footfalls 67, 69, 125
Foundations (of schooling) 59–62
Frame 19

Galvanism 50
German eggbutt bridoon 81
Girth tabs 82
Going 78, 146
Grand Prix 26;
  horse 48, 66
Grid work 91

Half halt 64, 66, 69
Half pass 115, 119–23, 138, 140;
  canter 123–5, 127
Halt 137–8;
  on long reins 151;
  on the lunge 143

Impulsion 60, 68

Jogging 44

Late
  behind 135–6;
  in front 136
Lateral work 77, 98, 100, 137;
  early 92–6
Leg yielding 92–4, 100
Longreining 67–8, 142–55, 150–1, 154
Loops, in canter 94–5
Loosening up 14, 59, 77
Lunge
  cavesson 142–3;
  line 13–15, 142–3;
  whip 142–3
Lunging 56, 75, 142–55;
  corrective 147, 150

Medium strides 104–7
Movement
  poor 19

Muscles
  rider's 43–4

Neck bend 66
Noseband 80
Numnah 51, 82–3

Osteopath 50–1
Outline 20, 60, 62, 72;
  in the walk 67–8

Paces 67–72
Packing 75–6
Passage 26
Piaffe 26, 60, 155
Pirouettes 66, 140–1
Planning 79, 141
Pole work 89, 118, 135, 147
Portraits 26–42
Posture 8–11
Prix St Georges 26
Progress
  assessing your 116–7
Props 71;
  for lunging 142
Protein 49
Pulse 49

Rag doll rolls 45
Record keeping 49
Rein back 111–2;
  improving 125;
  preparation for 97–8
Renvers 138–9
Respiration 49
Resting 129
Rhythm 62, 65, 69;
  in canter 95
Roadwork 52, 54, 57
Roller 56, 145

Saddle 51, 82;
  introducing the 145–6
Safety (in the arena) 55–6
Schooling
  early 57–62
Schoolmaster 94, 130, 136
Search (for a horse) 24–6

Selection 19
Serpentines 124, 139
Shoeing 52
Shoulder-in 100–104, 115, 116, 121, 138
Side reins 142;
 introducing the 145–6
Sideways leg stretch 46
Sideways stretch 45
Snaffle 80;
 cheek 81;
 rubber 81
Spurs 64, 116
Stance 20
Stiffness 65–6;
 in canter 71
Stomach tightening and spine stretching 46
Structuring work 58–9
Studs 75
Swimming 44

Teeth 50;
 wolf 50
Temperament 20, 22, 58
Temperature 49
Tempo changes 140
Tension 43
Test
 copy of 76
Thoroughbred 21
Three-time beat 69–70
Tooth gag 50
Topline 58, 67–8;
 building the 142;
 stretching the 89, 98
Tracks 55;
 in renvers 138–9;
 in shoulder-in 100
Training ground 55–6
Transitions 59, 65, 72, 87–8, 100;
 counter canter to trot 95–6;
 direct 113–4;
 to canter 70–1
Transport 76
Travers 114–6, 121, 138
Trot 24, 139, 145;
 collected 91–2, 137;
 extended 91–2, 137;
 medium 105–6, 137;
 working 68, 137
Tuition 11–12

Ultrasound 50

Veterinary surgeon 26, 50
Vices 20, 25
Video recording 13, 26, 73, 78
Visual aids 12

Waistline worker 45
Walk 22, 67–8, 96–7, 144;
 build-up to shoulder-in 102–3;
 collected 137;
 extended 105, 137;
 hurrying the 68;
 medium 105, 137
Way of going 22, 64
Weekly plan 59
Welsh cob 21
Welsh pony 66
Weymouth 82
Whip 64, 77, 98, 108, 131, 144
Whole body stretch 45
Working
 down 89;
 from the ground 97–8, 112;
 through the shoulders 122
Working-in 73
Worming 52

X point in arena 78, 97, 124, 139
X-ray 25, 26